PAPER FLOWERS

'We're dedicating this book to creativity and enthusiasm. To playing and to colours. To the beautiful and the aesthetic, the fun and the whimsical.
To magic and the desire to explore and have adventures.'

– Sine & Sara

PAPER FLOWERS

Sine & Sara Finne Frandsen

15 Stylish Projects to Make Your Own

Hardie Grant

QUADRILLE

Contents

Welcome

We are the sisters behind the creative flower studio, Almeja Space. We love flowers, colours and creating beautiful things, and it's our great pleasure to welcome you to our world of colour.

For us, flowers are pure happiness! They contribute beauty and positivity to their surroundings, and they put us in a good mood. When we give or receive flowers, something almost magical happens. The brain releases the 'love hormone' oxytocin, which helps to create a feeling of wellbeing, trust and connectivity. In addition, flowers stimulate your senses with their colours, shapes and textures. We find that the magic of flowers comes from the encounter between ourselves and the aura of the flowers, and we can become completely enchanted by them. That's why we do our absolute best to make sure our paper flowers work the same way.

We have designed 15 paper flowers especially for this book, each of which is our interpretation of a real flower. We are not trying to create an exact copy of nature, but instead we have challenged ourselves to play with colours, shapes and expressions. In our flower guides, we show you how to create the flowers yourself. You can follow these guides closely, or use them as inspiration to create your own totally personal flowers. Anything goes!

This book is an extension of everything we love, and we hope each and every page will inspire you: to create beautiful colour combinations, to immerse yourself, and to create and decorate with adventurous paper flowers. Creating paper flowers can feel like pure meditation, and it is perfect to do alone or in the company of those you love. So find some scissors and a glue gun, and let loose your creative side.

Welcome to our book!

Sine & Sara, Almeja Space

A WORLD

OF

PAPER FLOWERS

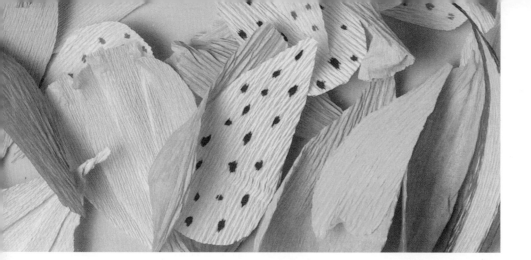

One day in March 2020, three rolls of crêpe paper suddenly turned into something beautiful and decorative – the first little Almeja paper flowers had come into the world.

We both fell in love with the idea that we could create flowers ourselves in exactly the colours and shapes that we wanted – preferably with lots of glitter. The reception on social media to our first flowers was completely overwhelming, and suddenly paper flowers became a big part of our lives. They were never intended to be sold, but there was a huge demand for them, and within 24 hours, our Almeja Shop was born. Our workshops began a few months later, teaching people how to make many different paper flowers. Several companies and private customers contacted us to ask for customised floral decorations – and who says no to that? So from having been impulsive creations, our paper flowers soon became part of our way of life. Flowers have always been dear to us, and we would be lying if we said we never buy fresh flowers – because we do. But paper flowers have also taken up a large place in our hearts, and we love how they hold endless possibilities in terms of colours, shapes and style.

Paper flowers are small, unique pieces of art that last forever. And they reflect the person who created them. Because even when everyone makes a flower following the same guide, the result always varies, as we each have different ways of working with materials, just as we interpret and visualise things differently. One variable is the colour scheme, which depends on the occasion and the individual's taste and mood. Another is the way in which we approach the whole process, and how we choose to arrange our flowers. Some may cut the leaves neatly and perfectly, while others prefer a more casual and organic look. But this does not make one flower more beautiful than another. On the contrary, it makes space for a variety of highly personal flowers, all of which are beautiful in their own way. We also see how the creative process is constantly changing. New paper flowers grow every day in our little studio in Copenhagen, and each unfolds in its own unique way. Our flower workshop, Almeja Space, is like our second home. Here, we can immerse ourselves in creativity; creative chaos is probably the best way to describe our workshop. So don't be afraid to make a mess at your desk. New ideas and colour combinations often arise precisely when colours and patterns are mixed up. Many of our colour combinations sprang up when the crêpe papers had been jumbled up and we could suddenly see how colours we otherwise would never have put together worked well with each other.

Almeja means 'clam' in Spanish. We think there is something unique and magical about clams. They open and unfold, like a flower blossoms. With that in mind, our ambition is that you are greeted with joy, colours and creative freedom the moment you step into our world of flowers. In addition, one of our mottos is: 'It should be fun to create.' When we make room for play and creativity, our ideas bloom. With this book, we hope to provide a creative outlet for you, and hopefully each page will inspire you to try your hand at using crêpe paper and colours in your own way.

Inspiration

When we develop new paper flowers, they are often inspired by nature with a twist of 'adventure.' Our flowers are not true copies of real flowers. We design them with a personal and aesthetic expression that we think is beautiful. And we get inspiration from many places: when we're on the go, visiting museums, flea markets or colourful markets in Southern Europe, in magazines, hidden in nature, the colours of the city, and immersing ourselves in our workshop. We have a tradition of going on an adventure every Wednesday to find inspiration. We hop on our cargo bikes and visit new places and areas around Copenhagen. One of the best places to visit is a flower market. It is a great sensory experience. Here, we soak up colours, shapes and even smells, and we often take photos of interesting details, colour combinations or stalls. This way, we can remember and be inspired by what we've seen at a later date. Botanical gardens are also an ideal place to visit for new inspiration and ideas for creating flowers. For example, the idea for our tropical Bird of Paradise was born in the Botanical Garden in Copenhagen.

There is also plenty of inspiration to be found in our parents' garden. All kinds of flowers shoot up in the summer – anemones, roses, lavender and the most beautiful hollyhocks. We love to explore and be inspired by the different varieties you can find around the garden. The beach is also a magical place to go for a change of scene. The sea, sand and dunes offer the most glorious colour combinations, and the plants and flowers that grow here are truly beautiful. In fact, ideas for new flowers can come from all sorts of beautiful places, such as in a random field of sunflowers on Bornholm, where the idea for our Baby Sunflower came to us.

When we design a paper flower, we may draw the individual parts it will consist of, or the whole structure. Many of our flowers are the result of experimenting, playing with composition, colours and shapes for the petals and leaves. The most important things for us are that it should be fun to create, and that you can't go wrong. The magic of crafting is that you decide how you want to express yourself.

Fascinating colours

We are both deeply fascinated by colours, and our main passion is to create joy and beauty with colour. That's why Almeja Space is one big burst of colour. Colours have the magical ability to instantly create a mood, awaken the senses and emotions, and boost motivation. In addition, we love how they can be combined in all sorts of ways in our paper flowers, creating very different looks.

When we need to find new colour combinations, we often explore our surroundings. We look at colours on façades and in architecture, patterns on wallpaper, posters and in works of art, covers of books and magazines – and, as previously mentioned, our desk is even a source of inspiration as colour schemes emerge from the messy scraps of paper. Finally, paint shops and colour swatches are a good place to find inspiration for new colours and colour combinations.

Colour composition comes naturally to some, but others require a little more focus to be able to see and find them. We'll tell you much more about this in our chapter 'Colours and paper flowers' (see p. 174).

'When we need to find new colour combinations, we often explore our surroundings.'

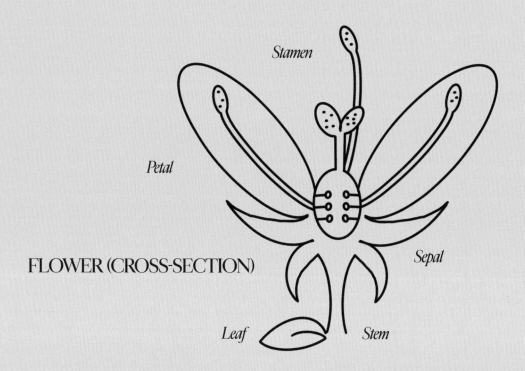

Stamen

Petal

Sepal

FLOWER (CROSS-SECTION)

Leaf

Stem

STAMENS

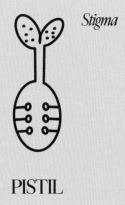

Stigma

PISTIL

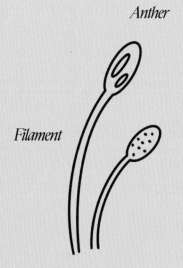

Anther

Filament

Anatomy of a flower

All flowers are different. And although our paper flowers are not a direct replica of those found in nature, they are still inspired by them and the way they are composed.

A typical natural flower consists of a stem, sepals, petals, stamens and pistil.

Pistil
This forms the core of the flower and we like to call this the eye of the flower.

Stamens
A stamen consists of a filament with an anther at the top. We often embellish the anthers on our flowers by dipping the tips in glitter or homemade confetti. Our stamens can be short, long or pointed (pp. 42–43).

Petals
The prominent and often colourful modified leaves around the central parts of the flower.

Sepals
The green leaves that sit just below the petals.

Stem
The long stalk which supports the flower heads.

Leaves
The green leaves attached to the stem.

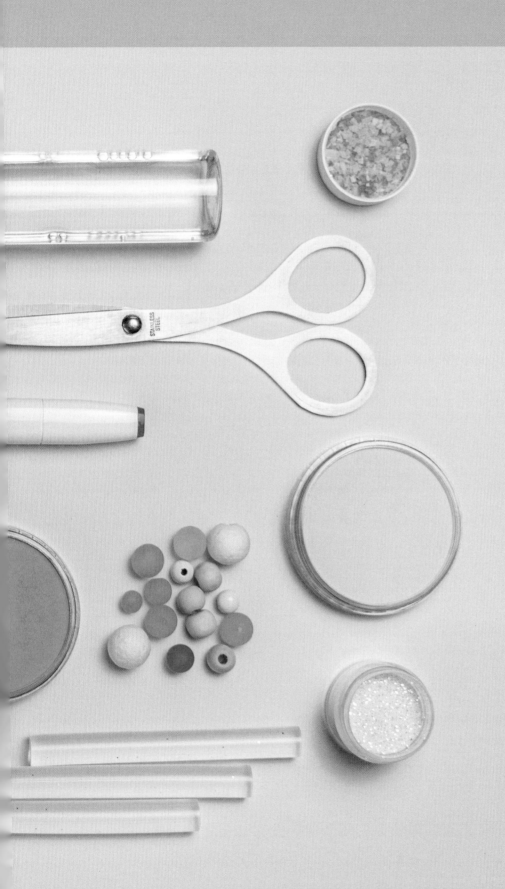

AND TOOLS

Introduction

To create your own paper flowers, you need certain materials and tools. We recommend you read through this section before you get started with your flowers. Then you'll have a greater understanding of what paper flowers are about and what you need to get together.

High-quality materials are essential, especially when it comes to crêpe paper. There are many different crêpe-paper manufacturers, and as with many things, the quality varies greatly. High-quality crêpe paper is easier to work with and keeps both its shape and colour better.

Another important tool is a glue gun. We have tested many glue guns and have come to the conclusion that it is worth paying a little extra. We have also found it pays to invest in some good scissors and wire cutters. It's highly personal which tools work best for you. Some people like scissors with small handles, others prefer larger ones. Some prefer a small cordless glue gun, while others like a sturdy glue gun best.

Here are our recommendations for materials and tools we cannot do without in our daily work with paper flowers. You can go and test the tools yourself and find the ones that suit you best.

Basic supplies

We recommend you start by getting:

- Crêpe paper. Don't buy anything under 60gsm as it will be too thin and difficult to shape. Our flowers are mainly made from paper weighing 60, 90 and 140 gsm

- Floristry wire in 0.9mm/19 gauge and 1.5mm/15 gauge thicknesses (also called hobby wire)

- Transparent craft glue

- Glue gun and glue sticks

- Good paper scissors (that you ONLY use for paper)

- Wire cutters

- Tracing or parchment paper (to copy the templates)

- Small containers for craft glue and possibly glitter

Additional supplies

If you want to go deeper and try out further techniques, we recommend you also get:

- Glitter in various colours

- Watercolour paints

- PanPastels

- Brushes

- Markers

- Beads or polystyrene balls

Crêpe paper

Crêpe paper is paper that has been specially treated and then 'crêped' to create the characteristic lines that run through it. These lines allow you to shape the paper in all sorts of ways.

All of our paper flowers are made from crêpe paper, and the best kind is Italian and FSC certified. Crêpe paper comes in endless colours, but you can go a long way by simply getting three or four different colours to start with. We love working with crêpe paper as it is a very forgiving, organic material that offers numerous possibilities. You will quickly discover how you can easily give it more life by stretching, bending and curling it in different ways.

Our flowers can be made with paper of all thicknesses, but they will have a different look depending on the paper you use. Therefore in each flower guide, we have given a recommendation of which paper thickness you should use. However, feel free to use a different thickness if that's what you have or if you want to experiment.

Thicknesses

When choosing your crêpe paper, as we mentioned, it's important to pay attention to the thickness. The thickness of Italian crêpe paper is indicated in grams per square metre, so pay attention to this when you're buying your paper. We work with three different thicknesses: 60 gsm, 90 gsm and 140 gsm. It's important you never choose anything under 60 gsm as it will tear easily when you work with it.

60 gsm: Over time, we have developed most flowers using 60 gsm crêpe paper. This thickness will give your flowers a very realistic look, and if you use pale colours for the petals, they can appear almost transparent. 60 gsm paper is also what we use if we want to colour the paper with other crêpe paper or watercolour paints (read more on pp. 56–57).

90 gsm: This type of crêpe paper is absolutely fantastic because it can be stretched a lot. The paper is crêped more finely and densely than 60 gsm and 140 gsm, and this makes it feel stiffer. This type of paper can be shaped in all imaginable ways, and we use it when we make curved leaves, for example for the Striped Orchid (see p. 152) or Cosmos (see p. 99).

140 gsm: This is the strongest paper we work with, and it's also the easiest to work with. You can quickly recognise a roll of 140 gsm paper as in addition to the vertical lines, it also has lines running horizontally. The first time you make a flower using 140 gsm paper, you may find it is a little more difficult to work with, especially when you're attaching the petals. It can be helpful to use a little extra glue and a little more force than usual when something needs to be attached. This crêpe paper holds its shape best, so if you want to make a lot of flowers that need to be transported, for example, it is clearly beneficial to use this paper. It is also the thickness we use when we cover the stem with crêpe paper (see pp. 50–51). Crêpe paper weighing 140 gsm does not take watercolour paints or wet dye well, so if you want to colour it, use markers and PanPastels.

60 gsm

90 gsm

140 gsm

As we said, crêpe paper is a very organic and forgiving material to work with. When you stretch it, it takes on a different texture and a slightly lighter colour. The photograph above shows how the different thicknesses of crêpe paper can stretch, and how the colour and structure can change accordingly. With each of these three colours, you can see two pieces of paper, one that has been stretched and one that hasn't.

Yellow: 60 gsm
Pink: 140 gsm
Coral: 90 gsm

Scissors

The most important tool of all is a proper pair of scissors made specifically for paper. There are, of course, many types of scissors to choose from, depending on how much and how finely you want to cut. But the most important thing is for the handles of the scissors to fit your hand so they are neither too big nor too small.

Glue

We work with two types of glue: an ordinary craft glue and a glue gun. We use craft glue to put glitter and confetti on the flowers and to cover the stem with crêpe paper. It dries a little slower than glue from a glue gun. We do not recommend using a glue gun to add glitter, confetti or crêpe paper to the stem as it dries too quickly, creates clumps of glue and can be seen too easily. We use a glue gun when the individual parts of the flower – the eye (flower centre), stamens, petals and leaves – need to be assembled. This glue dries after roughly 20 seconds, which makes it easier to continue working with the individual parts.

TIP } We recommend you invest in a good-quality glue gun, as these are generally easier to work with and stand better on the workbench.

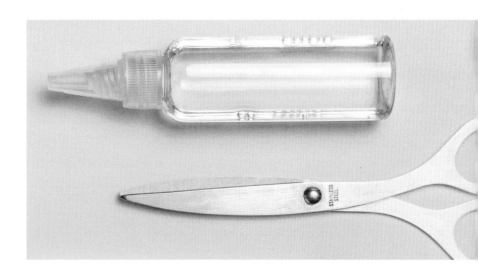

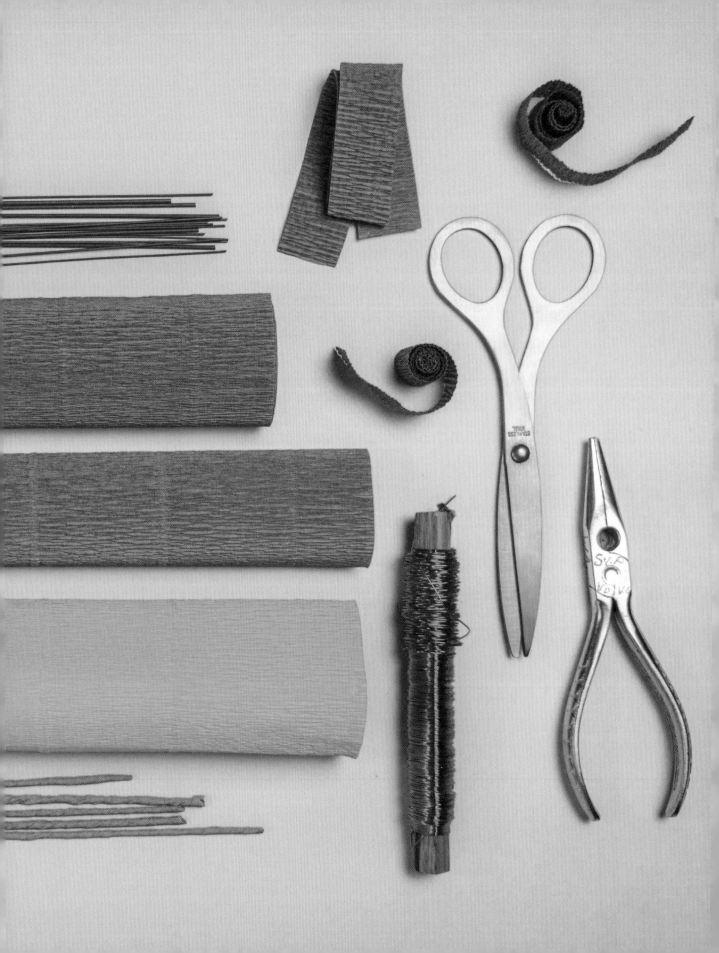

Floristry wire

You will need floristry wire to make the flower stems, which form the base of all of our flowers. Floristry wire is available in all kinds of thicknesses often referred to as gauge (ga). In this book, gauge refers to American Wire Gauge (AWG). You can easily find conversion tables for Standard Wire Gauge (SWG) online. We work with 0.9mm/19 gauge and 1.5mm/15 gauge wire. The average length of a flower stem is roughly 40cm/16in.

1.5mm: As a starting point, we always use floristry wire with a thickness of 1.5mm/15 gauge for our flower stems. The wire is relatively strong, but it can still be bent in various ways, which gives the stem a more lifelike appearance.

0.9mm: If you want to make a flower that bends naturally, or has a 'hanging effect' – for example Cosmos (see p. 99) or Fritillary (see p. 139) – use 0.9mm/19 gauge floristry wire. When you use floristry wire at this thickness, the flowers become much more flexible, creating a more vibrant look. We also use this thickness of floristry wire for flower shoots (see the Almeja Poppy, p. 73), and when making a flower with several branches such as the Baby Sunflower (see p. 93). It is easy to twist if you have to put several stems together. We also use it for the Trumpet Vine (p. 87), which consists of two flower heads twisted together.

TIP
As an alternative to thin floristry wire, you can use ordinary steel wire. You just need to be aware that it is a little tricky to manipulate and make perfectly straight. Therefore, steel wire works best for shorter sections, such as stems and offshoots.

Wire cutters

Wire cutters are indispensable, because you need them to cut the floristry wire. If you don't already have a pair in your toolbox, you can easily find them at any hardware store. Most wire cutters can be used, but it is a good idea to get a pair you find easy to hold.

Beads and polystyrene balls

It is always handy to have beads and polystyrene balls of various sizes. You need them to make the middle of the flower, what we call the eye of the flower. Maybe you already have some wooden beads or polystyrene balls lying around? If not, you can buy them in any craft store. The size of the bead determines how big the eye will be. You can always experiment with different sizes, but we often use beads that are 1cm/½in in diameter.

TIP   We recommend you get beads in white or neutral colours as then you can't see the colour of the bead through the crêpe paper used to cover them.

TIP } Get one or two PanPastels to try out and a marker pen or two. You can go a long way with these.

Markers and PanPastels

You can give your flowers extra colour, personality and variety by using markers or PanPastels. When you add colour to the leaves and petals, you create depth and vitality in the flower.

PanPastels are coloured pastels in plastic pots. The colours are highly pigmented for artistic quality. They are economical to use and you can cover large areas with very little colour. You use PanPastels by dabbing colour onto the crêpe paper with a sponge – the more you dab, the more intense the colour will be. This way, you can create both delicate and intense colours. You can decide for yourself whether the colour of the petals should be subtle and hazy in some places and more intense in others.

Markers are a little easier to control, and they typically produce deeper and brighter colours. We recommend you buy dual-tip markers that have a pointed tip at one end and a flat tip at the other.

Glitter

TIP } We recommend you only get one colour of glitter to start off with.

We love glitter because it adds extra life and sparkle to paper flowers – so remember to add glitter! You can dip either the stamens or leaves in it, creating a gorgeous effect. Glitter comes in all kinds of colours – we're majorly obsessed with gold glitter.

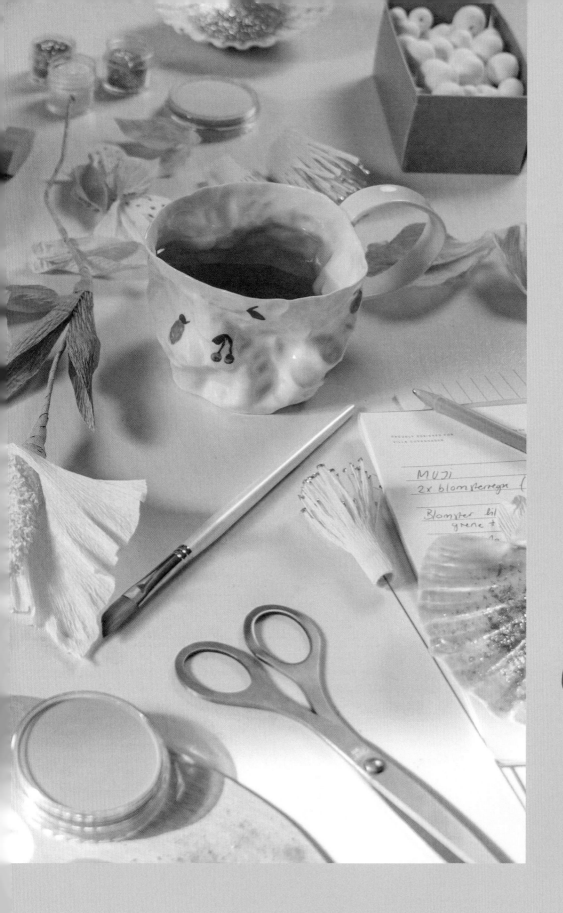

TECHNIQUES

Introduction

When we make paper flowers, we use a number of techniques to give the flowers life and an individual appearance – and these techniques are absolutely essential. Some are easy and others require a bit of skill – the best way to learn is to throw yourself into it and practise.

Do this a little before you start shaping the final flower parts, and you're more likely to get a great result.

We do not explain all the techniques in each flower guide, but instead reference these pages. We therefore recommend you read through this section before you start making your flowers.

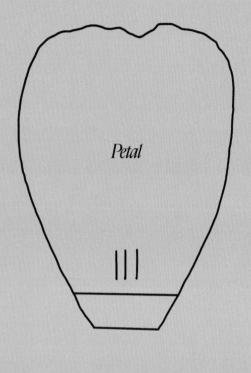

Petal

| | |

Templates

There are templates for all the paper flowers, which you will find at the end of each flower guide. The templates have a glue line indicating where you should place the glue, and the small vertical guidelines indicate which way the lines of the crêpe paper should run when you cut out the template. It is crucial that the lines run the right way when you are cutting the parts for your flower, as these are essential for shaping the crêpe paper correctly.

Here's what to do:

- We recommend you trace the templates by placing baking or tracing paper over them. You can then transfer the patterns to a piece of cardboard and cut them out. Then draw a glue line and the guidelines on the template. Now you're ready to cut the parts for your flower.

- Every template has a name – for example, 'Petal.' Remember to note down which flower each template belongs to in order to avoid confusion later.

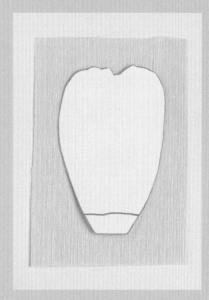

Cut the pattern pieces

When cutting the various elements of your flower, you can choose to cut each piece individually. You can also fold the paper twice or fold it several times. This way, you can cut multiple petals or leaves at once, which is smart if you have several flowers to make.

Here's what to do:

If you want to cut several petals or leaves at once, you can do it in the following way:

- First, cut a piece of crêpe paper measuring 50cm × 15cm (20in × 6in) (the lines of the crêpe paper should run along the longer length).

- Then fold the paper in half lengthways, and fold it lengthways once more so you have four layers on top of each other.

- Now fold the paper again, this time widthways. Now you have eight layers on top of each other and can cut eight leaves/petals at once.

Glue the petals on

We recommend you use a glue gun when
assembling your flowers. It is faster and gives a more
secure result, as the glue gun ensures all parts are
securely attached.

Here's what to do:
- As previously mentioned, the templates have a
  glue line indicating where glue should be applied.
  We recommend you only add a small amount of
  glue (about the size of a peppercorn), so the join
  isn't too big. And with the stamens, you also only
  need to apply a thin strip of glue.

Stretch and shape the petals

We use this technique for many of the leaves and
petals. It's an easy way to change a somewhat flat
and boring piece of crêpe paper into a more lifelike
petal. With this technique, you stretch the petal while
rounding it with your thumbs.

Here's what to do:
- Hold your index fingers and thumbs on either
  side of the petal – preferably at the widest point.
  Now pull on each side of the petal while applying
  pressure with your thumbs, 'rounding' the petal
  away from you. The petal should preferably be
  stretched most in the middle and still be gathered
  at the sides.

TIP Practise on some smaller pieces of paper before you shape your petals. This way you can get a feel for how much the paper can take before it tears. Should you end up tearing it anyway, you can cut a small curve in the petal so it looks like a natural part of its shape.

Twisted petals

Just as with the previous technique, you'll find we use the twist technique for a lot of flowers. The small twists in the top and at the edges of the petals add a beautiful effect and give the flowers life.

Here's what to do:
- First, stretch the paper at the edges. Hold the petal between your left index finger and thumb and use your right index finger and thumb to stretch the paper (or vice versa if you are left-handed). Imagine you are twisting the left side away from you and the right side towards you. Be careful not to tear the paper.

Curled petals

The curling technique gives petals a beautiful structure and adds lines up through the petals. We use it for the Almeja Poppy petals (p. 73), where we simply curl 2–3cm (¾in– 1¼in) from the bottom. Try it and see how easily you can give your petals more shape and structure.

Here's what to do:

- Once your petal has been stretched (p. 36), twist the entire petal together while pinching it so that the paper takes the shape of the twist. Don't be afraid of twisting it tight.

- When it is completely twisted, carefully unfold it again. The petal should now have a nice texture and a random fold at the top.

TIP } If you use 90 gsm crêpe paper, you don't need to stretch the petal first. It stretches by itself as you curve it.

Curved petals

You can use this curving technique to curl the petals inwards or outwards. It can also be used if you need to straighten petals and make them flat, as for the Baby Sunflower (p. 93). We also use the technique to give the flower the shape of a bell, as for the Fritillary (p. 139). Once you have tried the technique a few times, you'll find it is super easy to give the petal a nice shape. You can use it for both petals and leaves, as we have done with the Fritillary.

You will need a brush or a pencil to give the petal or leaf a curved shape. The tighter you hold the petal against the brush, the more curved it will be.

Here's what to do:

- Start by stretching the petal a little (for 60 gsm and 140 gsm – see the tip above if using 90 gsm paper).

- Hold the bottom of your petal, and place the brush handle approximately 1cm (½in) from the bottom.

- Now run the brush handle along the petal while you hold the petal firmly with your index finger on the back and your thumb on the front. The more you shape the petal with the brush, the more it will curve. Do this a few times until the petal has the right shape.

TIP } If you have run out of beads or
polystyrene balls, you can form
a ball of crêpe paper, which you
then cover with another piece
of crêpe paper and glue to the
floristry wire.

Eye (centre) of the flower

To make a nice and uniform coloured eye in a flower, cover a bead with crêpe paper. You can use any kind of beads (wooden, plastic or glass) or polystyrene balls. The bigger the bead, the bigger the eye. We recommend using a pale bead so it won't show through the crêpe paper used to cover it.

Here's what to do:

- Using a glue gun, add glue to the tip of the floristry wire and attach your bead.

- Cut a small piece of crêpe paper and stretch it so it is easier to shape.

- Now place the crêpe paper over the bead so the middle of the paper meets the top of the bead and 'shape' it around the bead.

- Twist the rest of the crêpe paper around the stem of the flower so it is tight and secure. You don't need to use glue to attach the paper to the stem.

Freestyle

You are more than welcome to use our techniques
and templates. But it can also be incredibly fun
to design your own flowers and develop your own
techniques. Try cutting different petals freehand and
see how they unfold as you shape them. Always
make sure you cut two identical petals so you have
a template you can save and use again if you like
the petal.

TIP   If you want more stamens, which
       can give a more compact look,
       you just need to cut more by using
       a larger piece of paper.

Stamens

Stamens can be made several different ways: long, short or pointed. We recommend you read through this and the following technique (see 'rolling stamens' on p. 44) before you start cutting your stamens.

Long stamens

- Cut a rectangular piece of crêpe paper (see the exact measurements on the templates for the different flowers and try, for example, the stamens for the Trumpet Vine on p. 87). Stretch it to double its width, and fold it in the middle of the narrower side.

- Hold the bottom of the paper with your index finger and thumb, then snip thin strips all the way down to your thumb (i.e. leave a piece at the end so the paper is not cut all the way through).

- When you have cut fine strips all across the paper, it needs to be 'rolled' – see p. 44.

Short stamens

- Cut a rectangular piece of crêpe paper (see the exact measurements on the template for each flower, and try, for example, the short stamens for the Almeja Poppy on p. 73). Stretch it to double its width, and fold it once in the middle of the longer side and then once again.

- Hold the bottom of the paper with your index finger and thumb, then snip thin strips all the way down to your thumb (i.e. leave a piece at the end so the paper is not cut all the way through).

- When you have cut fine strips all across the paper, it needs to be 'rolled' – see p. 44.

Pointed stamens

- A pointed stamen is a beautiful addition to the core of your flower – especially if you put glitter on it.

- Cut a rectangular piece of crêpe paper (see the precise measurements on the template for each flower).

- Stretch the paper and cut it into three strips. At the end of each strip, cut a small triangle/tip.

- Then hold the pointed part with your thumb and index finger, and rub the longer part so that it twists around. See how on the next page.

TIP { If you want a more raw and angular look, you can skip 'rolling' your stamens and just leave them flat.

Rolling stamens

We always 'roll' our stamens because it gives them a nicer, rounder and more cohesive look.

Here's what to do:

- After you've cut your stamens, unfold the paper so it is only folded once.

- Now use your index finger and thumb to roll the stamens. To do this, hold the base of the paper strip with one hand and roll the rest of it back and forth between the finger and thumb of your other hand. Remember to apply pressure so the paper holds its shape. The more you roll, the finer the stamens become.

Placement of petals

All our flowers have several shapes of petal, and how many you use and where you place them has a huge effect on their final look. Here, we introduce you to the different techniques you can use depending on how you place the petals on your flowers.

When placing your petals, remember that no two flowers are alike. Natural flowers are only very rarely perfect or symmetrical, so it doesn't matter if a petal is a little crooked – you can always add an extra one or leave the flower as it is.

Symmetrical placement of petals

To make it easy to place the petals, we work with a symmetrical technique where we glue two petals at once. However, the result doesn't have to be completely symmetrical – again, remember that in nature, flowers are neither symmetrical nor perfect.

TIP } If you want an even fuller flower, you can easily get one by adding more petals. Cut the desired number of extra petals and place them where you think it suits the flower best.

Flowers with four petals

Here's what to do:

- Start by gluing two petals opposite each other.

- Then glue the next two petals. They should be placed directly opposite each other in the spaces between the first two petals.

- When the first four petals are attached, 'open' the flower by bending the four petals downwards (see the technique on p. 49).

Flowers with eight petals

If your flower needs to have eight petals, attach the first four petals as previously described, and then continue with the next four.

Here's what to do:

- Once the flower has been opened, there will be some natural spaces between the petals, and this is where the remaining four petals should be placed. The last four petals should always fill the spaces between the first four.

Flowers with five petals

Several of our paper flowers have only five petals, for example the Baby Sunflower (p. 93) and Cosmos (p. 99). However, they need to be placed in two different ways, as the petals are different sizes.

With the first technique, the five petals are placed so that the sides just touch each other and the ends meet at the bottom.

Five petals – compact:
In this technique, the five petals only just touch each other.

Here's what to do:

- Start by gluing a petal on.

- Glue the next petal so it sits right next to the first, but without going over it.

- Continue like this until all five petals have been glued.

- Open the petals and let the flower unfold.

Five petals – overlapping:

In this technique, the petals overlap each other.

Here's what to do:

- Start by gluing a petal on.

- Glue the next petal on so it overlaps half of the first petal.

- Continue like this until all five petals have been glued.

- Now open the flower so the petals sit nicely around the middle of the flower.

Open the flower

Once you've glued all the petals on, it's time to unfold the petals and open the flower.

Here's what to do:

- Place two fingers on top of a petal and gently press down where it is glued.

- Continue around the flower until you have unfolded all of the petals.

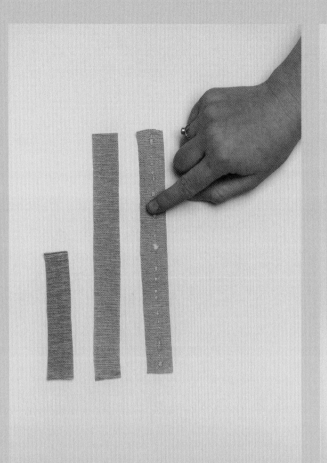
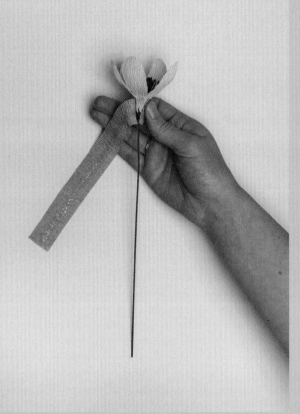

Covering the floristry wire

Once you have finished your flower, you need to cover the stem with crêpe paper. We have chosen to cover all our flower stems and shoots with crêpe paper weighing 140 gsm as it gives a really beautiful texture to the stem. You have the option of choosing any colour for your stem if you cover it in crêpe paper – it doesn't necessarily have to be green.

In our flower guides, we have primarily used different tones of green crêpe paper for the stems – for example, a light green for the Bird of Paradise Flower (p. 81) and a darker green for many of the other flowers. For the Wheat Shoot, the petals and the stem have the same colour, which gives it a very tranquil appearance (p. 119).

It can be challenging to cover the stem with crêpe paper for the first time. So we recommend you practise with some floristry wire before you start on your finished flower.

You will need craft glue and a rectangular piece of 140 gsm crêpe paper that measures 34cm/13in long by 2cm/¾in wide.

Here's what to do:

• Cut a piece of crêpe paper using the template on p. 173 and stretch it to about twice its size. Remember that the lines in the crepe paper should run across the width of the strip, not down its length.

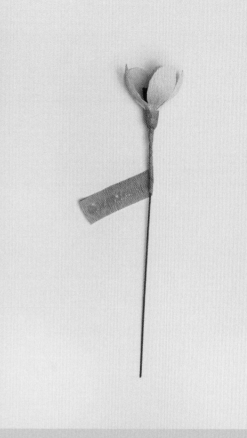

- Add a thin strip of craft glue down the middle and spread it out with your finger. You only need a small amount of glue as the crêpe paper quickly absorbs it, and if it gets too wet, you will be unable to work with it.

- Start from the top, where all the petals are glued. Wrap the crêpe paper around the flower – preferably three or four times. Pull tight and press the paper firmly with your fingers.

- When the crêpe paper is securely attached at the top, you can start to twist it down the stem.

- Place the crêpe paper at a slight diagonal across the stem. Hold the top of the stem with your right hand.

- Now twist the stem around with your right hand, while you hold the stretched crêpe paper with your left hand. This way, the paper will be twisted around the stem. Work your way down the stem while pressing the paper firmly against it with your right hand.

Note: The measurements on the templates for the stem are for guidance. You may need an extra piece to cover the whole stem.

TIP } If you want to give your flower a more imaginative look, you can cover the stem with a colour other than green. For example, use yellow, light blue or pink.

Add the leaves to the stem

Many of our paper flowers only have a few green leaves. Not because we don't like them, but because we think it gives more focus to the flower itself, and it creates a lighter individual flower and bouquet. There are no rules for whether a flower must have leaves or not, so you can always just try them out. Experiment with various shapes of leaves, and add more to your flower if you want to.

Decide for yourself which colour leaves your flower will have. We are pretty fond of the delicate olive green colour. You'll find a range of templates for different green leaves on pp. 172–173.

Here's what to do:

- First, cover the stem with crêpe paper (see p. 50).

- Cut your leaves using your chosen template.

- Shape the leaves. See the stretching technique on p. 36 and the twisting technique on p. 37.

- Add glue with the glue gun and stick your leaves on the stem.

- Finish by hiding the joint between the leaves and the stem with a small piece of green crêpe paper in the same colour as the rest of the stem.

TIP By making leaves in different shades of green and various shapes and sizes, you can play and give life to the bouquet or individual flower.

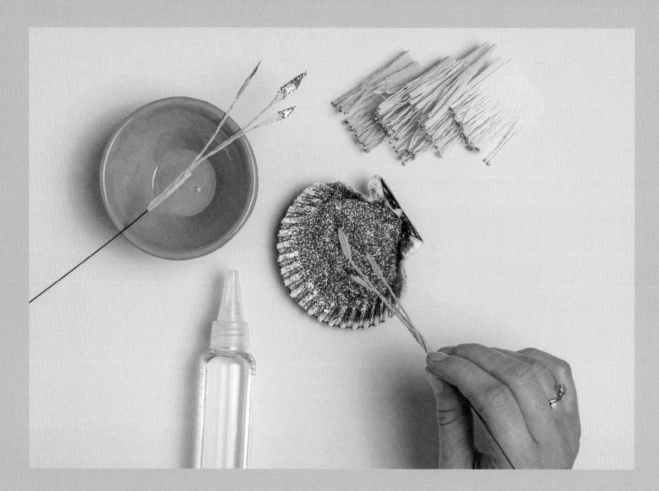

Glitter

Add glitter to the end of your stamens to give your flowers an enchanting look. We love glitter and often use gold glitter on the tips of our stamens.

You will need:
- Glitter in your colour of choice
- Bowl of craft glue
- Completed stamen

Here's what to do:

Lightly dip your stamen (see how to cut them on pp. 42–43) in craft glue and then into the bowl of glitter.

- Let it dry – it's best if the glitter glue doesn't touch any surfaces, so let the stamen dry over a glass, dish or bowl.

Paper confetti

If you want your flowers to have a more gentle and natural look, you can decorate the stamens and the centre of the flower with confetti made from crêpe paper. You can even make the confetti yourself, so you can choose which colour it will be. It can also look cool if you mix a bit of glitter into the confetti.

You will need:

- Bowl of craft glue

- 1 finished stamen in your chosen colour for the paper confetti

- 1 finished stamen in your chosen colour to decorate with the paper confetti

Here's what to do:

- Make two stamens – one to be cut into confetti and one to have confetti added to (see pp. 42–43).

- Fold one stamen and cut tiny pieces from it into a bowl or another container.

- Dip the other stamen in craft glue and then in the bowl of confetti.

- Set aside to dry.

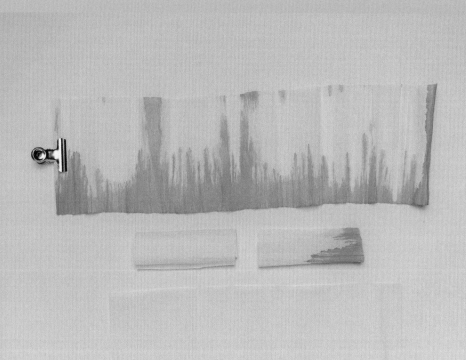

Dyeing

The colours of crêpe paper are very beautiful in themselves, but you can also colour your crêpe paper to get the exact colour to suit the flowers you are going to make.

You can colour your pale crêpe paper with watercolour paints or with crêpe paper that has a darker and more intense colour. It works best to dye 60 gsm or 90 gsm crêpe paper as they take the colour better. We love colouring white or light beige crêpe paper with a bolder colour such as orange, yellow or pink.

You will need:

- One piece of pale crêpe paper, max. 90 gsm, that measures 50cm/20in by 11cm/4in for eight petals. The lines on the crêpe paper need to run parallel to the short side.
- Either a small piece of 60 gsm crêpe paper in a darker and more intense colour to colour the water with, or watercolour paint.
- A little bowl of water (the water should be approximately 2cm/¾in deep).
- A waterproof surface (e.g. wax cloth or plastic bag).

Note: As it can be messy to colour your crêpe paper, we recommend you place a wax cloth or plastic bag underneath it while you work.

Here's what to do:

- To colour with crepe paper, place a small coloured piece of crêpe paper into the bowl of water and stir with a spoon so the water takes the colour. If you want a more intense colour, you can add more crêpe paper.

- To colour with watercolour paints, wet a brush and stir it into the watercolour paint. Dip the brush into a bowl with water and mix so the water takes the colour.

- Now take your rectangular piece of crêpe paper and roll it up – it may curl.

- Carefully dip the crêpe paper into the bowl of coloured water. The paper will absorb it quickly, so only leave it there for 1–2 seconds.

- Unfold the paper and lay it out to dry on a waterproof surface.

- Once the paper has dried, it is ready to be folded for you to cut petals from it.

TIP You can also dye your crêpe paper with tea instead of watercolour paint or crêpe paper if you want earthy tones. This gives the flowers a more subdued look.

TIP } You can also draw lines with a
marker pen along an entire petal –
or leaf – to make it stripy.

Markers

Many real flowers have spots and stripes of various sizes and thicknesses, and you can easily give your petals an extra touch by using markers to draw similar spots and stripes. We recommend you use a marker pen in an intense colour to ensure a bold effect. We use a regular artist marker pen that has a thin tip at one end and a wide tip at the other.

If you want to draw small spots and thin stripes, choose a marker with a small, fine tip. For large spots, choose a marker with a large tip, and if you prefer wide stripes, you need a marker with a wide tip.

Note: Do not shape your petal until you have drawn on it with a marker. If you do, it won't quite have the right effect.

You will need:
- Your petals
- A marker pen in your chosen colour
- A waterproof surface

Here's what to do (spots):

- Start at one end of the petal and gently dot the marker pen all over it. If you want the petals to have a subtle look, you can choose to add spots with lots of space between. If you prefer a more intense look, you can add lots of spots close to each other.

- Allow your petals to dry before shaping them.

Here's what to do (stripes):

- Colour the edge of your petal with a marker pen and repeat on the remaining petals. Be careful not to touch the petal before the marker pen dries, otherwise the colour will smudge.

- Allow your petals to dry before shaping them.

PanPastels

PanPastels provide an artistic aesthetic. The consistency is very similar to an eyeshadow, and the colour is very intense and long lasting, so you don't need to put a lot of colour on your sponge to create an effect on the petals. You can paint on paper weighing 60 gsm, 90 gsm and 140 gsm. In general, you get the best result by adding paint to light crêpe paper, but, of course, it depends on the PanPastel colour you use.

Note: PanPastels rub off easily, so put something underneath while you work.

You will need:
- Your pre-cut petals
- A sponge
- A PanPastel in your chosen colour

Here's what to do:

- Have your pre-cut petals ready.

- Lightly dip the sponge in your PanPastel.

- Take a petal, hold it at one end, and lightly dab or paint it with the sponge.

- You can repeat the process if you want a more intense colour. Otherwise, you can stop here and continue with the rest of the petals.

- Be careful not to touch the area where you have applied the PanPastel too much as it will easily rub off. The colour never really dries, but sits on the petal, a little like eyeshadow.

Taking care of your flowers

Your paper flowers will last (almost) forever, and if you look after them well, they will continue to look as they did when you first made them. We have gathered our best tips on how you can easily look after your flowers so they retain both their shape and colour.

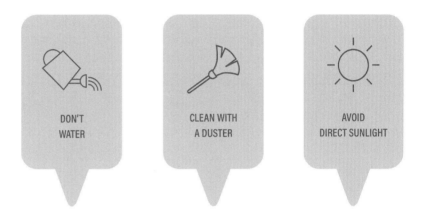

DON'T
WATER

CLEAN WITH
A DUSTER

AVOID
DIRECT SUNLIGHT

Storage
If you get tired of having your flowers on display, we recommend you pack them away and store them in a box. This way, you can easily find them again, just as you would with Christmas and Easter decorations. It's always a good idea to fold the petals so that the head of the flower is protected as much as possible.

Crumpled flowers
Flowers made of crêpe paper are reasonably hardy, especially if they are made of stronger crêpe paper such as 140 gsm. If your flowers do become crumpled anyway, you can easily unfold them and adjust the petals and stem without damaging them.

Avoid direct sunlight

If the flowers are exposed to direct sunlight for a long time, they will fade, so avoid placing them on the windowsill, or make sure to move them around a little so they are not constantly exposed to sunlight.

Give them new life

If your paper flowers have been out for a long time and become exposed to sunlight, you can quickly give them new life by covering the stem with new crêpe paper over the top of the old. If you have made flowers without leaves on the stem, you could also add a few leaves.

Different heights

We often end up making most of our flowers on the same type of floristry wire, so they are the same height. However, they can be easily adjusted by cutting some of the length off. The floristry wire can also be bent or twisted at the bottom so the flowers fit into the vase you want to use for them, or you can extend the stem by twisting two lengths of floristry wire together and then covering them with crêpe paper so you can't see the join. This way, you can create exactly the height you want.

FLOWER

GUIDES

Introduction

We have created 15 beautiful paper flowers based on some of our favourite flowers in nature, and there is something for everyone. Some are from Danish summer meadows, some we spotted in Tivoli Gardens, some have tropical vibes and some are just classics. All the paper flowers have been made so they can be displayed alone or in a bouquet, and they can all be combined.

Each of the 15 flowers is graded using a key of small flower symbols indicating the level of difficulty:

= easy

= medium

= advanced

If you haven't made paper flowers before, we recommend you start with one of the easier flowers. And remember, it's a good idea to read through the techniques before you start making your flowers.

At the end of each of the 15 flower guides, you will find templates for all the parts that make up that individual flower. Read more about how to use the templates on p. 34.

Go wild!

We have made more than 800 Almeja Poppies, and it always surprises us how beautiful and enchanting they are.

The Almeja Poppy is our signature flower. It is an interpretation of the iconic poppy that can be found on verges around the Danish summer countryside. There are more than 100 species of poppy, and plenty of them grow wild in Denmark.

We love poppies because they remind us of the summer. We think poppies are suited to dyed crêpe paper, as it gives the flowers a very life-like effect. In this guide we've shown you an orange version, but it can be equally beautiful in beige, pink or yellow.

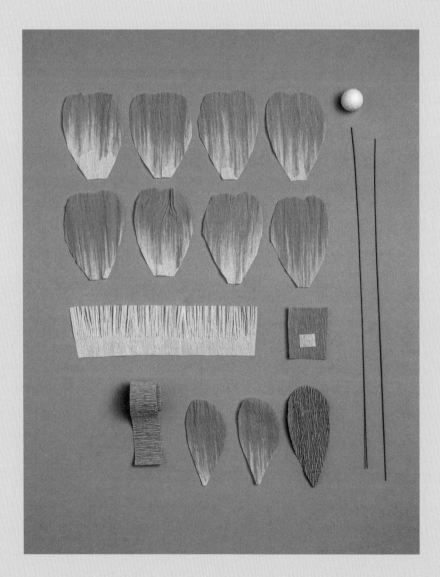

YOU WILL NEED:

1 piece of floristry wire for the flower stem,
L: 40cm/16in, T: 1.5mm/15ga

1 piece of floristry wire for the stem of the bud,
L: 30cm/12in, T: 0.9mm/19ga

1 bead for the eye (centre) of the flower

1 piece of crêpe paper for the eye of the flower, 60 gsm

1 piece of crêpe paper for the anther, 90 gsm or 140 gsm

1 stamen, 90 gsm or 140 gsm

8 petals, 60 gsm

2 petals for the flower bud, 60 gsm

1 sepal for the flower bud, 140 gsm

Crêpe paper to cover the two stems, 140 gsm (see p. 173)

Small container of glue and another of glitter

DYEING THE CRÊPE PAPER

For this flower, we have dyed 60 gsm crêpe paper using the technique on p. 56. To get the orange colour, we dipped white crêpe paper in water dyed with orange crêpe paper (you can also use watercolour paint). You can, of course, choose to use single coloured crêpe paper for the petals. They are beautiful in delicate pink or orange-red, for example.

1. Glue the bead to the end of the 40cm/16in floristry wire. Once it has dried, cover it with crêpe paper (see p. 40). Now cut the stamens, and make sure to 'roll' them so they are fine (p. 43 and 44).

   Now attach the stamen: Place it in front of you on the table, add a thin strip of glue with a glue gun around the stem. It can be helpful to add a little glue at a time, so it doesn't dry before you finish rolling.

2. When the stamens are glued on, you can 'open' the eye of the flower by unfolding the stamens and gathering all the tips so they sit nicely all the way around the eye of the flower. You gather the tips by 'pressing' them together, so they don't stick out in different directions and look messy.

   Now add glitter to the tips:
   First, lightly dip the stamen tips into craft glue – they should only just touch the glue. Then dip them carefully in glitter (or confetti) (pp. 54 and 55). Set them aside to dry in a vase.

3. While the stamens dry, you can shape your
    petals. You do this by using the twisting
    technique (p. 37), stretching technique (p. 36)
    and curling technique (p. 38). When the petals
    are curled, carefully unfold them. Remember,
    you can always shape the petals further once
    they are glued on.

4. When all the petals are shaped, glue them in
    pairs with a glue gun (see p. 36 and 47) until you
    have attached all eight petals. You can unfold the
    bottom of the petals a little so they are not too
    pinched after you have gathered all the ends.
    Set the flower aside in a vase.

5. The next step is to make the flower bud. Shape the two petals in the same way as the petals of the flower: twist, expand and curl them. Then glue them opposite each other on the 30cm/12in piece of floristry wire.

6. When the petals are attached, glue a single green sepal on. Shape the sepal by using the twisting technique (p. 37) and stretching technique (p. 36).

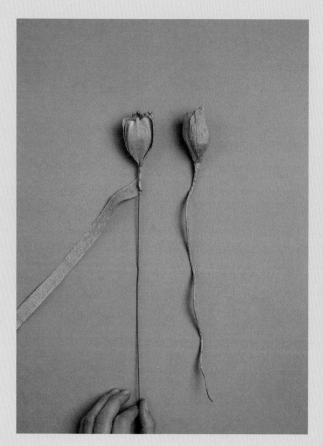

7. Now the stem needs to be covered with crêpe paper. Cut a strip of crêpe paper roughly 1cm/½in wide and 15cm/6in long – remember the lines of the paper should run widthways. Cover the floristry wire of theflower bud by using the technique on p. 50.

8. Before covering the stem of the poppy itself with crêpe paper, you need to make an anther to be glued to eye of the flower. Shape a small piece of crêpe paper by twisting the top and rolling it up. Add a little glue with a glue gun to the bottom of the anther and stick it in the middle of the eye of the flower. Then cover the floristry wire with crêpe paper.

Finish by giving both pieces of floristry wire a few kinks so the flower and the bud look more lifelike.

ALMEJA POPPY
– TEMPLATES

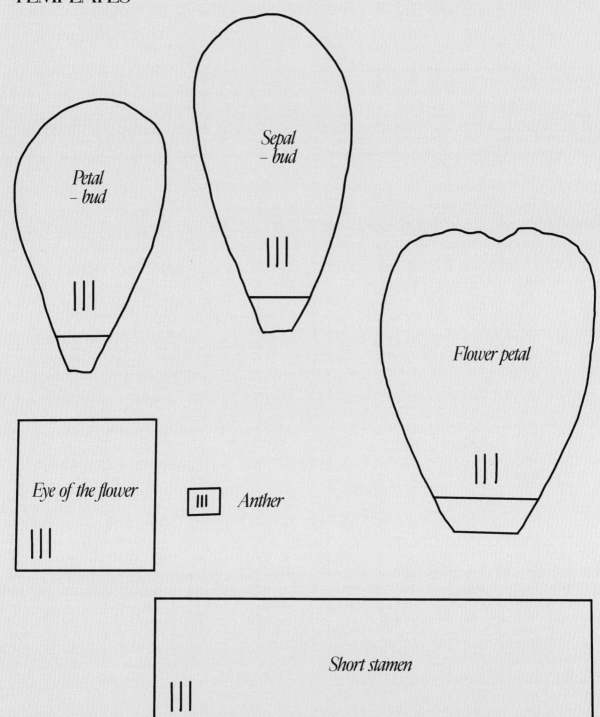

Petal
– bud

Sepal
– bud

Flower petal

Eye of the flower

Anther

Short stamen

Bird of Paradise flowers remind us of blue seas, warm sun and bright skies.

The Bird of Paradise Flower is a tropical plant originally from South Africa and the Canary Islands. The plant can be found in many living rooms, but often without the flower itself.

The Bird of Paradise Flower can easily be displayed on its own, and it looks great if you have an odd number – just one or three – in a vase. It works well if you put rice in the pot or vase that you're arranging the flowers in. The rice works a bit like floral foam, making sure the flower stays put (see pp. 198–199).

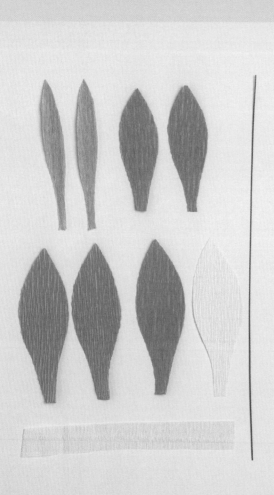

YOU WILL NEED:

1 piece of floristry wire for the stem, L: 40cm/16in, T: 1.5mm/15ga

2 inner petals, 90 gsm

2 small petals, 140 gsm

3 large petals, 140 gsm

1 leaf, 140 gsm

Crêpe paper to cover the stem, 140 gsm (see p. 173)

1. Shape the two inner petals by stretching them (p. 36). Then glue them to the floristry wire opposite each other (p. 36 and p. 46).

2. Shape a small and a large petal and glue them to the back of the flower.

3. Then shape another small and large petal, and glue them to the front so that the two small petals are opposite each other on the right, and the two large petals are opposite each other on the left.

4. Add the third large petal below the two large ones you have glued on the left. This petal should be placed so it hides the join of the two petals.

5. Shape the leaf by stretching it (p. 36), and glue it on under the two small petals on the right.

    Now all the parts are attached, cover the stem with crêpe paper, preferably in the same colour as the leaf (p.50).

6. Shape the stem by bending it in different places.

BIRD OF PARADISE
- TEMPLATES

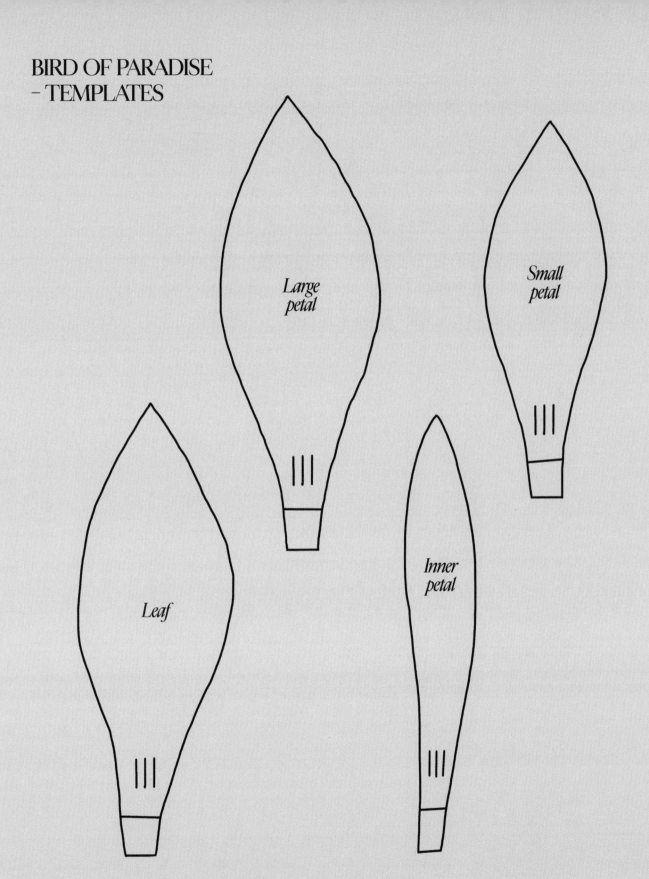

Large
petal

Small
petal

Leaf

Inner
petal

Playful and joyful
    – and beautiful
in all kinds
    of colours.

The Trumpet Vine is a vine creeper that can grow up to 5–8 metres/16–26 feet high. The name describes the shape of the flower, which resembles a trumpet. The genus consists of two species: the one from North America grows well in Denmark, while the other, native to China and Japan, can only grow indoors over here.

You can give the flower different looks depending on whether it bends upwards or downwards. The Trumpet Vine is joyful and a really good choice if you want to create height in your bouquet, or if you want flowers that droop down over the side of your vase. They are also beautiful alone, as the head itself consists of two flowers.

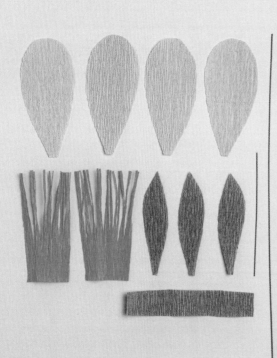

YOU WILL NEED:

2 pieces of floristry wire, L: 15cm/6in, T: 0.9mm/19ga

1 piece of floristry wire to lengthen the stem, L: 40cm/16in, T: 1.5mm/15ga

2 long stamens, 140 gsm

4 petals, 140 gsm

3 leaves, 140 gsm

Crêpe paper to cover the stem, 140 gsm (see p. 173)

Small container of glue and another of glitter

Note: The Trumpet Vine consists of two flower heads joined together. This means you need to make two flowers at the same time.

1. Start by making the two flower heads. First, cut the two long stamens that will form the core of the flowers (p. 42). After you have 'rolled' them, add glitter to the tips. Carefully dip them in craft glue and then in glitter (p. 54).

   Let them dry for a few minutes before gluing each to a short floristry wire with the glue gun.

2. While the stamens dry, cut and shape your petals. They should have three twists in the top of each one (p. 37) and be stretched at the widest part (p. 36).

   Once the petals have been shaped, glue them to the stamens on opposite sides (p. 36 and p. 46). Note: there should only be two petals on each flower head.

TIP } If you are making several Trumpet
Vines, you can curve the heads of
some of them and leave the rest
standing straight up. This gives a
nice effect to your bouquet.

5. Then cover the twisted stem and your extra floristry wire with green crêpe paper (p. 50).

6. You can choose to bend the flower head before you lengthen it with the extra floristry wire.

7. Twist on your extra floristry wire to make the stem longer. Then glue the final green leaf on.

8. Cover the join of the two stems with crêpe paper. Start where the top two leaves have been glued on, so that the end of the leaves are covered with crêpe paper.

3. Now the two flower heads need to be twisted together. Lay them on top of each other so they form a cross, and twist the two stems together into one.

4. Once the stems are twisted together, add the leaves. Shape two of your green leaves by giving them a single twist at the top (p. 37) and then stretch and shape them (p. 36). Now glue a leaf onto each side, so that they cover the join of the two flower heads.

TRUMPET VINE
– TEMPLATES

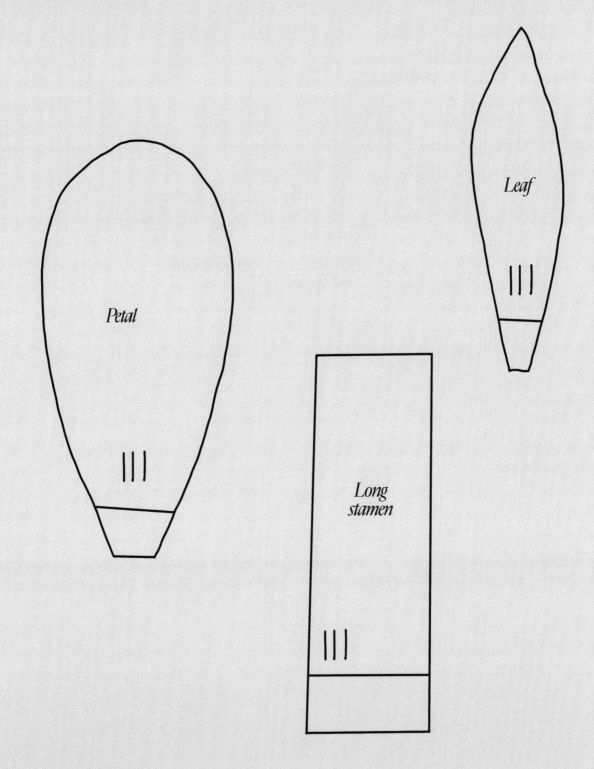

Leaf

Petal

Long
stamen

Summer and sunshine together in one flower.

This trio of flowers is inspired by sunflowers, although sunflowers are in the aster family and usually have only one large flower. We have interpreted it here as a mini version. The colour can range from light yellow to dark red with a black, orange or brown middle.

Baby Sunflowers are beautiful alone, but can also give a nice depth to a bouquet of single flowers. You can also make a variant with only two flower heads and play with the colour combination.

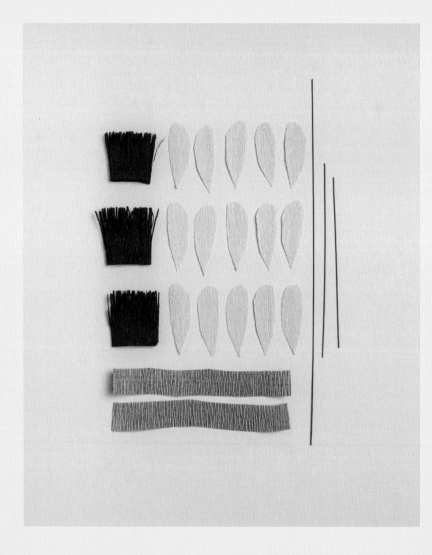

YOU WILL NEED:

1 longer piece of floristry wire,
L: 30cm/12in, T: 1.5mm/15ga

2 shorter pieces of floristry wire,
L: 15cm/6in, T: 0.9mm/19ga

3 short stamens, 60 gsm

15 petals, 140 gsm

Crêpe paper to cover the stems,
140 gsm (see p. 173)

Note: This sprig has three small flower heads. It's a good idea to make the three flowers at once.

1. First, cut your short stamens (p. 43) and roll them (p.44). They should measure roughly 1.5cm/⅝in in length and may be slightly ruffled. If they are longer, you can cut them so they don't stick out too far between the petals.

2. Then the stamens need to be glued onto floristry wire: Place a stamen on the table in front of you, add a thin strip of glue with a glue gun, then roll the stamen around the floristry wire. Repeat with the other two stamens.

3. Now you should shape your petals by stretching them – at the top too if you like (p. 36). The petals should be relatively flat, so if they curve too much after you have stretched them, straighten them out with a brush (p. 39).

4. When the petals are ready, they need to be glued to the core of the flower following the technique 'flower with five petals – compact' (p. 48).

5. Now your flower stems are ready to be covered with crêpe paper and assembled. Start by covering the longest stem with crêpe paper – it should reach about a third of the way down the stem (p. 50). Also cover one of the short stems with crêpe paper. Twist them together and cover the twist with crêpe paper.

6. Cover the final short stem with crêpe paper and twist it onto the other two. It should be placed approximately two-thirds of the way down the stem. Cover this twist with crêpe paper, too.

7. Once your flower is completely finished, you can bend the stems and the flower heads until they look the way you want.

BABY SUNFLOWER
– TEMPLATES

Petal

Short stamen

Simple but beautiful, and one of our absolute darlings.

Cosmos aren't just beautiful flowers – they also attract insects and butterflies. Its evenly spaced petals are the reason it got its name. It comes from the Greek word 'kosmos' which means 'harmony.'

Our summer Cosmos is sophisticated in its simplicity and elegance, and it can create lightness in a mixed bouquet or be used in a hanging display.

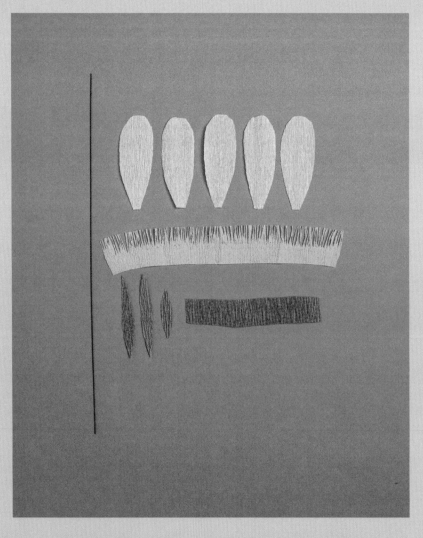

YOU WILL NEED:

1 piece of floristry wire,
L: 40cm/16in, T: 0.9mm/19ga

5 petals, 90 gsm

1 short stamen, 90 gsm or 140 gsm

2 large leaves, 140 gsm

1 small leaf, 140 gsm

Crêpe paper to cover the stem,
140 gsm (see p. 173)

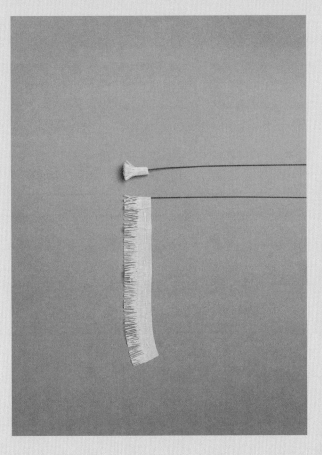

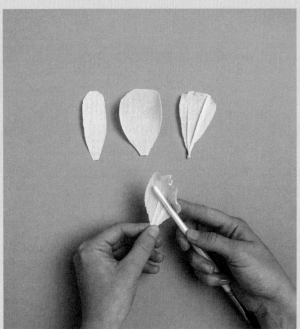

1. Cut the stamen following the technique on p. 43.
    Then glue it onto the floristry wire as follows:
    Add a line of glue to the stamen with a glue gun
    and roll it around the floristry wire. It helps to add
    the glue a little at a time, so it doesn't dry before
    you have finished rolling. The stamen should be
    tight and compact, and measure approximately
    1.5cm/⅝in long. If it becomes too long and not
    full enough, you can trim it.

2. Cut out the five petals, then stretch them (p. 36),
    make two folds in each petal (see photo), and use
    a brush to curve them (p. 39).

3. Once all five petals are shaped, glue them to the
    middle of the flower using the technique 'flower
    with five petals – overlapping' (p. 49).

4. The next step is to cover the floristry wire with crêpe paper (p. 50). Once the stem is covered, the leaves need to be attached. Shape the three leaves – two large and one small – by stretching them (p. 36).

   Place them on the stem so the smaller one sits just under the petals, one large leaf sits a little further down, and the other one is placed roughly halfway down the stem.

5. Hide the joins of the leaves and the stem by covering them with more crêpe paper.

6. Give the stem a few bends, and curve close to the flower head so it gets a nice drooping effect (see the photo on p. 98).

COSMOS
– TEMPLATES

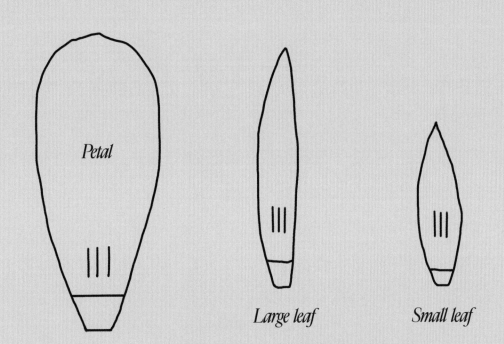

Petal

Large leaf

Small leaf

Short stamen

The Hollyhock is a pure Danish summer idyll.

The Hollyhock is a hardy plant with large, brightly coloured flowers that look like roses, and heart-shaped petals. It blooms extensively from July to October in Denmark, and is a real treat for bumblebees. The Hollyhock exudes peace and tranquility, and is ideal if you want to create a romantic look.

YOU WILL NEED:

1 piece of floristry wire, L: 40cm/16in, T: 1.5mm/15ga

5 small petals, 140 gsm

8 large petals, 140 gsm

1 triangle of crêpe paper for the pistil, 140 gsm

1 short stamen for confetti (same colour as the pistil)

2 leaves, 140 gsm

Crêpe paper to cover the stem, 140 gsm (see p. 173)

Small container of craft glue

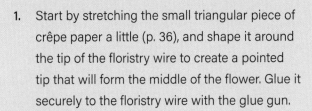

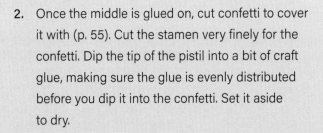

1. Start by stretching the small triangular piece of crêpe paper a little (p. 36), and shape it around the tip of the floristry wire to create a pointed tip that will form the middle of the flower. Glue it securely to the floristry wire with the glue gun.

2. Once the middle is glued on, cut confetti to cover it with (p. 55). Cut the stamen very finely for the confetti. Dip the tip of the pistil into a bit of craft glue, making sure the glue is evenly distributed before you dip it into the confetti. Set it aside to dry.

3. Now you need to shape all the petals. To do this, twist them twice at the top of each side (p. 37), and then stretch and shape them (p. 36).

4. Once the petals have been stretched, they should be glued to the middle of the flower with a glue gun. Start by gluing the five small petals using the technique 'flower with five petals – overlapping' (p. 49).

5. Then attach four of the large petals, placing them opposite each other in pairs (p. 36 and p. 47).

6. Now the remaining four large petals need to be glued on in the spaces between the first four (p. 47).

7. Now all the petals have been attached, it's time to cover the floristry wire with crêpe paper (p. 50).

Once the stem is covered, the two green leaves need to be attached. Shape them first by giving them a couple of twists at the top and then stretching them (pp. 36–37). Stagger them on the stem and finish with extra crêpe paper so you can't see the joins.

Now your Hollyhock is finished, and you just need to give the stem a few bends to give the flower a more natural look.

HOLLYHOCK
– TEMPLATES

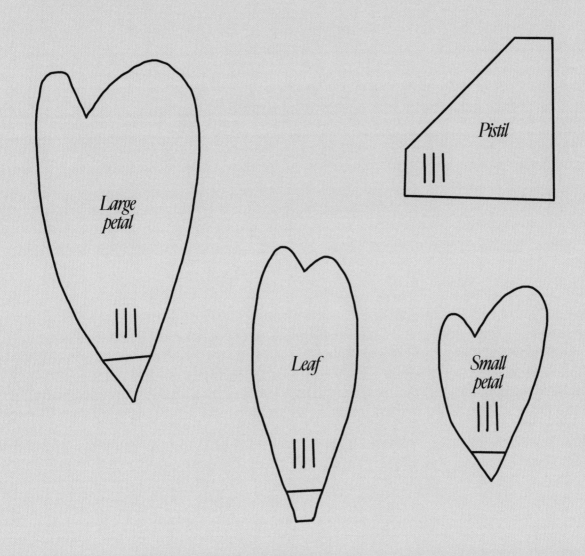

Pistil

Large
petal

Leaf

Small
petal

Short stamen for confetti

Popular, distinctive and often brightly coloured. Here, in a more gentle pale colour.

The botanical name for the Flamingo Flower is *Anthurium*. This flower has been a popular houseplant in recent years, and we're big fans of it, too. The heart-shaped petals can be white, salmon, rose, orange or red. The flower comes from warmer climes and was first discovered in South American rainforests.

The Flamingo Flower is highly decorative and can be made in all sorts of colours. It works well in our *flora* decorative concept where the stem is coiled at the bottom so it can stand up by itself. Make several flowers using our *flora* concept to create your own little meadow (see p. 201).

YOU WILL NEED:

1 piece of floristry wire,
L: 40cm/16in, T: 1.5mm/15ga

1 triangle of crêpe paper for the middle,
140 gsm

1 stamen for confetti, 140 gsm

1 large petal, 90 gsm

2 leaves, 140 gsm

Crêpe paper to cover the stem,
140 gsm (see p. 173)

Small container of craft glue

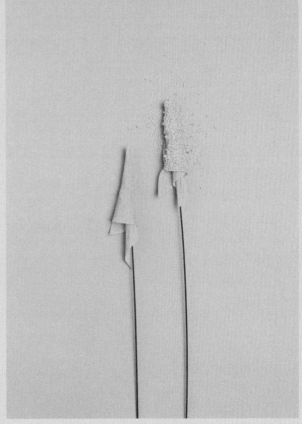

1. Start by shaping the middle of the flower from the triangular piece of crêpe paper. Pay attention to which way the lines run in the paper (see the template) as this is crucial for you to be able to shape it. Stretch the paper slightly (p. 36), add a line of glue with a glue gun, place your floristry wire 1cm/½in inside the crêpe paper, and roll the paper around it so it forms a pointed cylinder. Add glue along the side, so the paper is firmly attached.

2. Once the middle of the flower has been shaped, you need to add confetti. The confetti is made by cutting small pieces from your stamen (p. 55). Carefully apply the craft glue to the entire middle of the flower, and then gently dip it into the confetti. Set the stem aside to dry.

3. Now you need to shape your petal. It only needs to be expanded a little at the bottom so it can reach all the way around the middle of the flower. It should also have five small twists on each side towards the tip (pp. 36-37).

    Once the petal has been shaped and the confetti is fairly dry, you can glue on the petal. Add a thin line of glue with a glue gun at the bottom of the petal and fold it around so that it crosses over itself at the front.

4. Now the flower stem needs to be covered with crêpe paper (p. 50).

5. Then two green leaves should be glued to the
   stem. Shape them by stretching them at the
   widest part (p. 36). Glue the two leaves about
   a third of the way from the top – note that the
   leaves need to face each other (p. 52). Cover the
   join between the leaves and the stem with a little
   extra crêpe paper.

   Now your Flamingo Flower is finished, and all
   you need to do is bend the stem so that it fits
   the vase or bouquet it will be placed in.

FLAMINGO FLOWER
– TEMPLATES

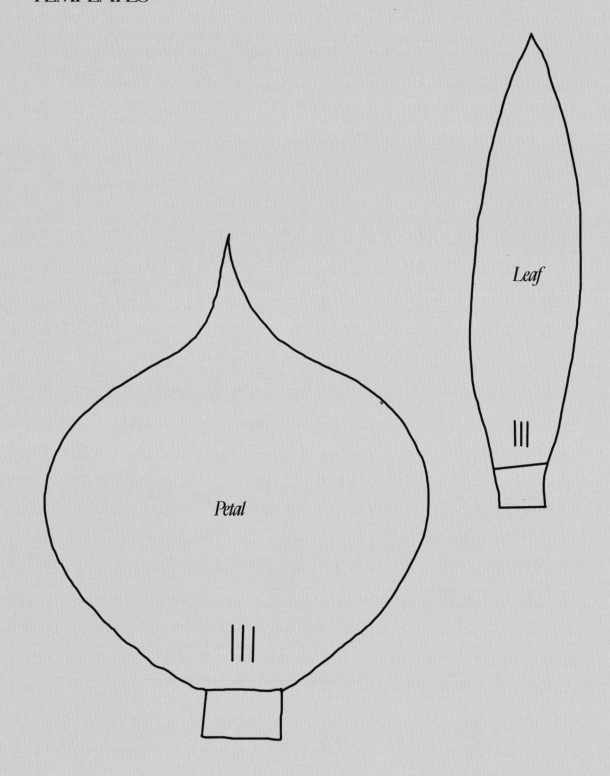

Leaf

Petal

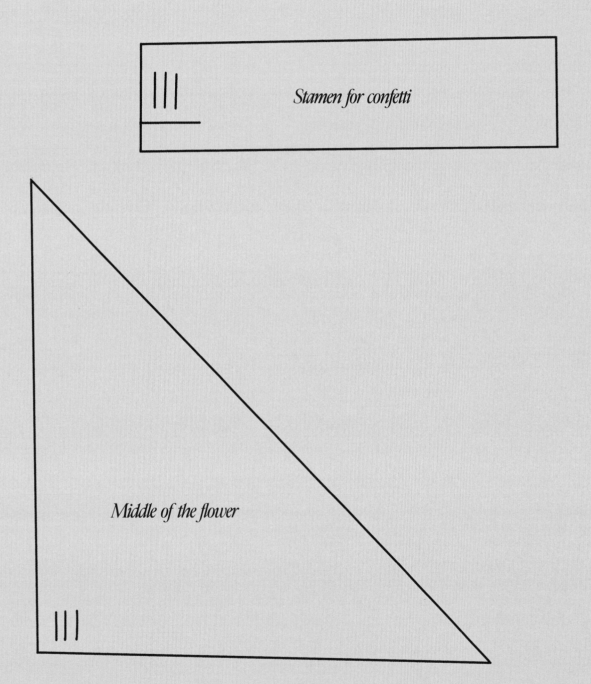

Stamen for confetti

Middle of the flower

A piece of the Danish summer countryside.

Wheat is one of the most farmed cereals in the world, and it was one of Denmark's very first cultivated crops. Our wheat shoots can be used as a decoration for many celebrations throughout the year. We have made an enlarged shoot of wheat that works best if you use a single colour. The wheat shoot can be used as a 'filler flower' in a bouquet of paper flowers instead of flower shoots or leaves.

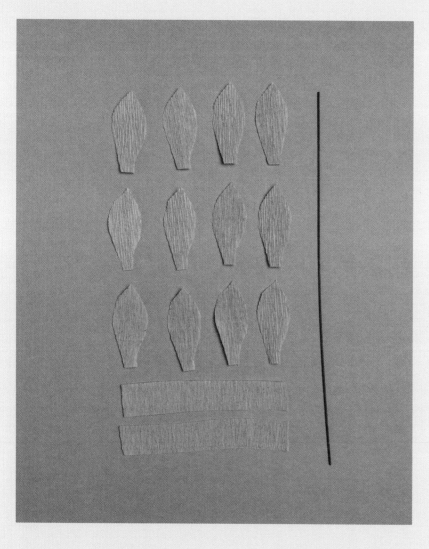

YOU WILL NEED:

1 piece of floristry wire,
L: 40cm/16in, T: 1.5mm/15ga

12 kernels, 140 gsm

Crêpe paper to cover the stem, 140 gsm

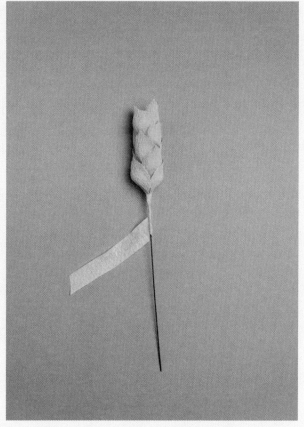

1. Shape the 12 kernels by stretching them at the widest part (p. 36).

   Now the kernels need to be glued to the floristry wire. Start by gluing two kernels opposite each other (p. 36 and p. 47). Rotate the floristry wire 90 degrees and glue two more kernels a little further down, so they cover the joins of the first two kernels. Continue like this until all 12 kernels are glued on.

2. Cover the floristry wire with crêpe paper – preferably in the same colour as the kernels (p.50).

TIP } Wheat shoots work well in light orange, but also look good in green if you want to use them as a filler flower.

3. If you want to make a larger or smaller version of our wheat shoot, you can cut the kernels in different sizes and experiment with either fewer or more kernels. This way, you'll get non-identical wheat shoots, which will add a natural and more realistic appearance.

WHEAT SHOOT
- TEMPLATES

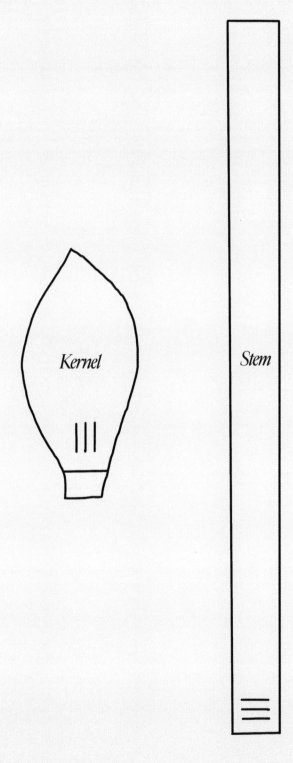

Kernel

Stem

Meadow Buttercups pop up in April and let us know that spring is on the way.

This buttercup's botanical name is *Ranunculus acris*, but is better known as the Meadow Buttercup. It grows wild in Denmark, and when the first flowers appear, it's a sign spring has arrived. Meadow Buttercup petals are always yellow, and we have chosen to make our version in a warm and fresh yellow.

The Meadow Buttercup is ideal as a napkin ring to dress the table, but also stands beautifully alone in a little vase.

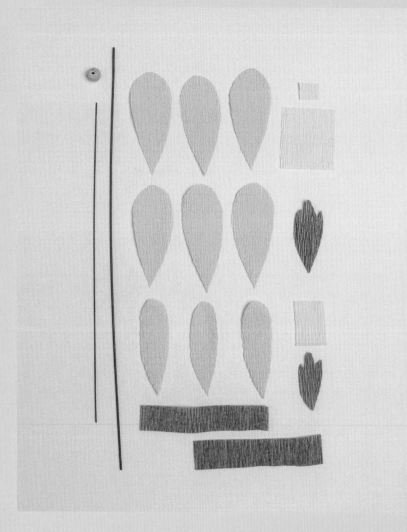

YOU WILL NEED:

Main flower

1 piece of floristry wire,
L: 30cm/12in, T: 1.5mm/15ga

1 bead for the eye (centre) of the flower, approx. 1cm/½in

1 piece of crêpe paper for the eye of the flower, 90 gsm

1 piece of crêpe paper for the anther

6 large petals, 140 gsm

1 leaf, 140 gsm

Crêpe paper to cover the stem, 140 gsm (see p. 173)

Small container of glue and another of glitter

Small flower shoot

1 piece of floristry wire, L: 15cm/6in, T: 0.9mm/19ga

1 small piece of crêpe paper for the eye of the flower, 90 gsm

3 small petals, 140 gsm

1 small leaf, 140 gsm

Crêpe paper to cover the stem, 140 gsm

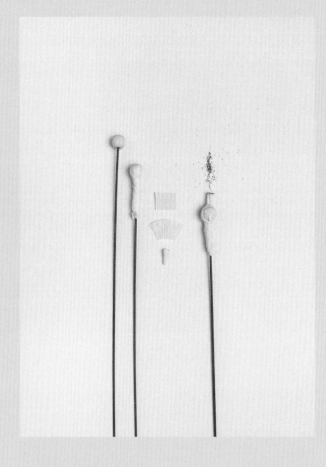

1. Start by making the main flower. Glue the bead to the end of the floristry wire. Take the piece of crêpe paper for the eye, and stretch it out to cover the bead. Then take the small piece of crêpe paper and shape it as shown in the photo, stretching the top of the paper and rolling it around itself so you have a small anther that is wider at the top than the bottom. Now glue the anther onto the top of the bead with a glue gun. If you want to add glitter, you can dip the tip into a small amount of craft glue and then in glitter.

2. Next, shape the six petals for the main flower. They need to have two twists in the top (p. 37) and then be stretched (p. 36). Once shaped, glue them down just below the bead. Start by gluing the first three petals on so they sit very tightly around the bead. When you look at the flower from above, you should only be able to see the bead and not any of the stem of the flower. Then glue the remaining three petals on in the spaces between the first petals.

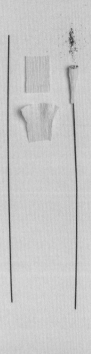

3. Now we'll make the small flower. Start by shaping the small piece of crêpe paper as shown in the photo. The paper should be shaped in the same way as the small anther on the other flower, but glued directly onto the floristry wire. Stretch the top part of the paper, and apply glue from the glue gun to the part that isn't stretched. Glue the paper to the floristry wire by rolling it around the wire. Then dip the tip in craft glue and then a small amount of glitter (p. 54).

4. Now the three small petals need to be shaped in the same way, by making two twists at the top of each one and then stretching the petals. Glue the petals around the middle of the flower so that approximately 1cm/½in of the anther sticks up out of the middle.

5. Before joining the flowers together, cover the two pieces of floristry wire with crêpe paper (p. 50). Note: the main flower should only be covered about a third of the way down the stem. When both stems are covered, twist them together. Twist the small flower stem around the stem of the main flower roughly a third of the way down, and continue to cover the rest of the stem with crêpe paper.

If the stem is too long, you can just cut it to the length you want it to be.

6. Now the two leaves need to be glued to the stems. Shape them by stretching them, and attach the large leaf where the two stems meet. The small leaf should be placed in the middle of the stem of the flower shoot. Then bend the stems a little so they aren't completely straight.

MEADOW BUTTERCUP
– TEMPLATES

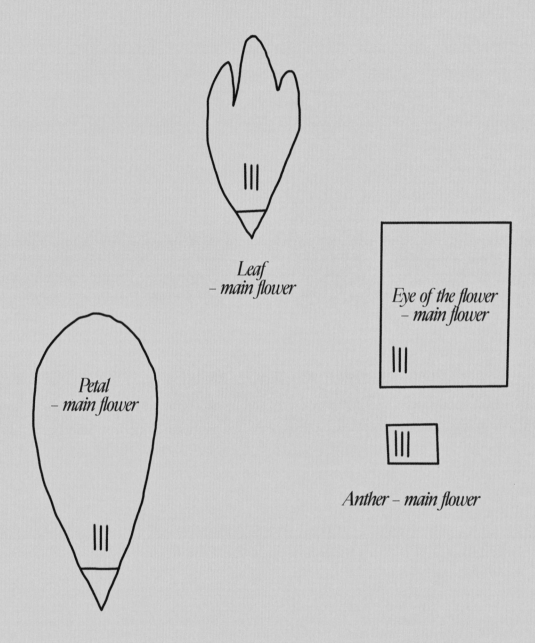

Leaf
– *main flower*

Eye of the flower
– *main flower*

Petal
– *main flower*

Anther – *main flower*

*Petal
– small
flower*

*Leaf –
small flower*

*Eye of the
small flower*

A sophisticated flower oozing spring vibes and simplicity.

The Almeja Spring Flower is made up of white petals, a discreet brown eye (flower centre) and beautiful sunshine-yellow stamens. If you put several together, you'll have an abundant white bouquet. We have made the flowers without glitter or confetti on the stamens and have given them a tousled and casual look instead.

For this version, we used two different types of floristry wire to make the stems extra long. We used 0.9mm/19 gauge for the flower itself, and an extra piece of 1.5mm/15 gauge floristry wire to lengthen and create a nice and natural 'drooping effect'.

The Spring Flower can also be made as a shorter version where you make the flower on 1.5mm floristry wire.

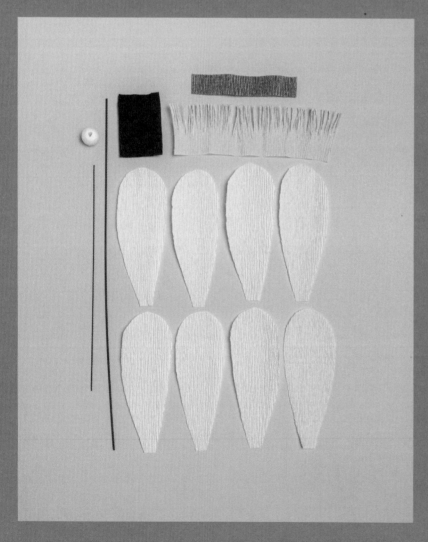

YOU WILL NEED:

1 piece of floristry wire,
L: 20cm/8in, T: 0.9mm/19ga

1 piece of floristry wire to lengthen the stem, L: 40cm/16in, T: 1.5mm/15ga

1 bead for the eye (centre) of the flower

1 small piece of crêpe paper for the eye of the flower, 60 gsm

1 short stamen, 140 gsm

8 petals, 140 gsm

Crêpe paper to cover the stem, 140 gsm (see p. 173)

1. Glue the bead to the end of the floristry wire.
   Now the bead needs to be covered with crêpe
   paper to form the eye of the flower, so take the
   small piece of crêpe paper, stretch it and cover
   the bead with it (p. 40).

   Then glue the stamen firmly around the bead
   (p. 43). The bottom of the bead should meet
   where the strips of the stamen begin. Imagine
   the uncut part of the stamen is placed under the
   bead so that the stamens form a circle around
   the eye of the flower. When the entire stamen
   is glued on, press round it to make sure it is
   properly attached.

2. Now your eight petals need to be shaped. You do
   this by giving the petals three twists at the top
   (p. 37) and stretching them (p. 36).

   Then they need to be glued onto the stamen,
   starting with the first four petals. They should
   be glued in pairs opposite each other (p. 47).
   Then add the remaining four petals in the spaces
   between the first.

3. Now both pieces of floristry wire need to be covered with crêpe paper (p. 50). Then they need to be joined together. This is done by twisting approximately 3cm/1¼in of the thin floristry wire (the one the flower is attached to) around the top of the thick floristry wire. Start approximately 3–4cm/1¼–1½in down the thicker floristry wire. Then cover the join with crêpe paper so you can't see where the wires are joined.

4. The final step is to bend the head and the stem of the flower so the flower has the right hanging effect. You could also shape the upper part of the stem around a bottle – you'll get a nice curve that way.

ALMEJA SPRING FLOWER
– TEMPLATES

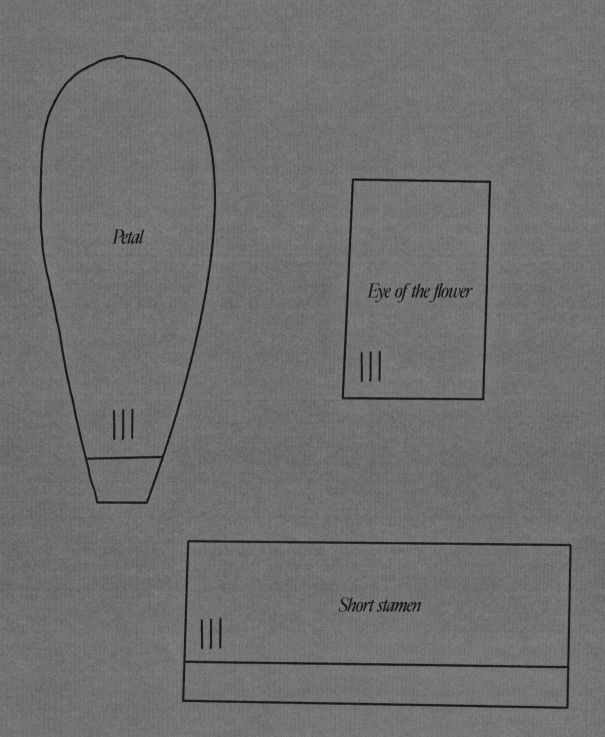

Petal

Eye of the flower

Short stamen

Fritillaries could be flowers from Alice in Wonderland.

The Fritillary grows from a bulb and always attracts attention in the garden – it's so adorable and has the cutest little spots. The flowers look like little bells, hanging beautifully from the stem. The flower is quite unique and without a doubt a very special sight – whether it's alone or displayed in your bouquet. Fritillaries grow wild in many parts of Europe.

With its pale blue petals with orange spots, our version is more adventurous than natural fritillaries. They are beautiful by themselves and can easily be displayed singly or as part of a flower arrangement.

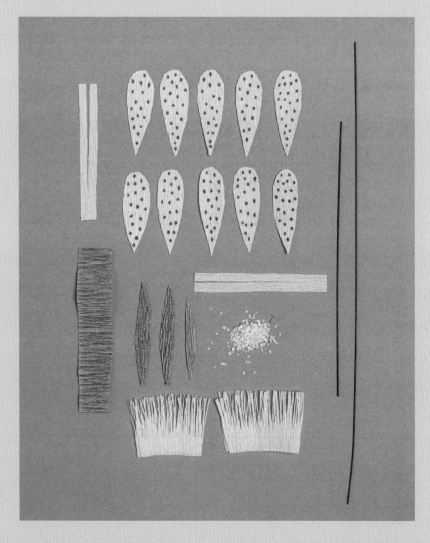

YOU WILL NEED:

1 piece of floristry wire,
L: 30cm/12in, T: 0.9mm/19ga

1 piece of floristry wire,
L: 20cm/8in, T: 0.9mm/19ga

2 long stamens for the middle,
90 gsm or 140 gsm

2 short stamens, 90 gsm or 140 gsm

1 stamen for confetti, 90 gsm or 140 gsm

10 petals, 140 gsm

2 large leaves, 140 gsm

1 small leaf, 140 gsm

Crêpe paper to cover the stems,
140 gsm (see p. 173)

Marker pen for making spots

Brush to shape the petals

Small container of glue

Note: Fritillaries consist of two flowers that each sit on a piece of floristry wire. Here we show you how to make them at the same time.

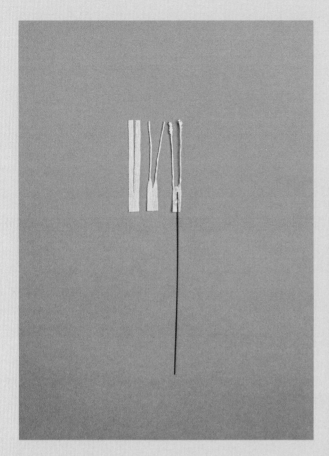

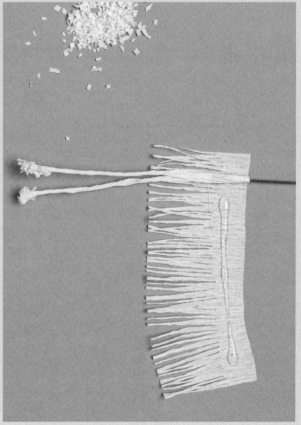

1. Start with the two long stamens that will form the middle of the Fritillary. Stretch the crêpe paper and cut it down the middle, leaving about 1.5cm/⅝in at the bottom uncut. Now roll the two pieces you've cut so they are round (p. 44).

Now add the confetti to the tips. First, make a short stamen in the same colour as the long stamens and cut it into confetti (p. 55). Dip the tips of the long stamens in craft glue and then in the confetti.

When the stamens are dry, they each need to be glued to a piece of floristry wire. Place the stamens on the table, apply lines of glue with a glue gun, and place the floristry wire on top. Roll the stamens around the floristry wire and press down so they are firmly in place.

2. Cut the short stamens and roll them so they look nice. Now they are rolled, they need to be glued to the floristry wire where you have glued the two long stamens. Once the short stamen is glued, the long stamens should stick out approximately 3–4cm/1¼–1½in at the top.

3. Now it's time to start on the petals – five for each flower.

    Add small spots to them with a red or orange marker pen. Preferably use a marker pen with a pointed tip.

    Then the petals should be stretched a little (p. 36) and curved over a brush (p. 39) so they are flat and wide.

    Now the petals need to be placed around the middles of the flowers. There should be five petals on each (p. 48). Start by gluing a petal on. Glue the next petal so it sits right next to the first, but without going over it. Continue like this until all five petals are glued on.

Open the petals and let each flower unfold. The petals should curve so they form a little bell around the core of the flower.

4. Cover both flower stems with crêpe paper (p. 50). It should go to about a third of the way down the stems. Then twist the stems together and continue to put crêpe paper on the twisted stem. Now bend both flowers so that the heads hang down. You can shape them around something cylindrical so that the curve is nice and even.

5. The final step is to add the three green leaves. First, shape them by stretching them and then curving them with a brush – just like you did with the petals.

Glue one large leaf where the two flower stems join. Then glue the second large leaf to the middle of the left flower stem. The small leaf should be glued roughly halfway down the right flower stem.

TIP } Remember that you can always play with colour combinations and give your petals spots in other colours. You can also leave the spots off and make uniform coloured petals as we've done here with this dark blue version.

FRITILLARY
– TEMPLATES

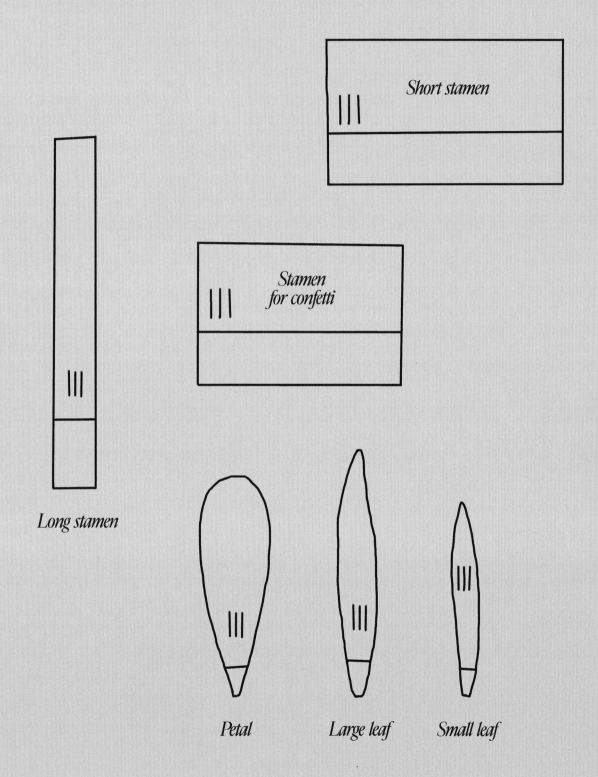

Short stamen

Stamen
for confetti

Long stamen

Petal

Large leaf

Small leaf

*Small, elegant
and perfect
as a table decoration.*

Our Mini Anemone is an elegant little flower, and a good place to start if you haven't made paper flowers before. You can easily vary its appearance by mixing colours, and they are perfect table decorations for Easter, Christmas and weddings.

We recommend you make them on floristry wire that is easy to bend, for example 0.9mm/19 gauge. You can then use them as napkin rings or as standalone *flora* displayed on the table, or combine them with other flowers to create your own little meadow right on your dining table.

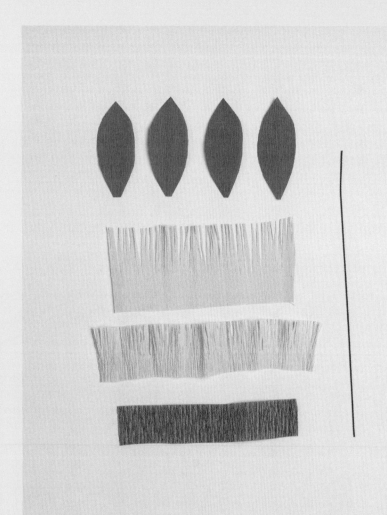

YOU WILL NEED:

1 piece of floristry wire, L: 25cm/10in, T: 0.9mm/19ga

1 short stamen for the middle of the flower, 140 gsm

1 long stamen, 140 gsm

4 petals – 60 gsm, 90 gsm or 140 gsm

Crêpe paper to cover the stem, 140 gsm (see p. 173)

Small container of glue and another of glitter

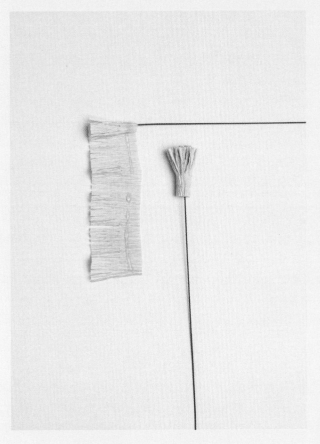

1. The first thing you need to do is cut the short stamen that will form the middle of the flower (p. 43). It should measure approximately 1.5–2cm/⅝–¾in. Glue it to the floristry wire. You can trim it after you have glued it to the floristry wire if it's too long.

2. Now glue the long stamen onto the short stamen, then open the middle of the flower so that the long tips of the stamen form a nice circle around it. Next, carefully dip the tips in craft glue and then in glitter. Set aside to dry.

3. While the glitter dries, shape your petals. This is done by stretching them at their widest part (p. 36).

   Glue the petals symmetrically around the part of the stamen that hasn't been cut (p. 36 and p. 47). Once the flower has been assembled, you should only be able to see the cut part of the stamen when you look into the flower.

4. Now cover the stem with crêpe paper (p. 50).

   Finish by giving the stem small bends so it is not perfectly straight.

MINI ANEMONE
– TEMPLATES

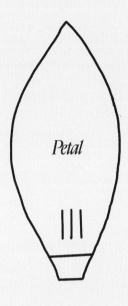

Petal

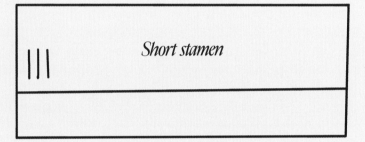

Short stamen

Long stamen

*A flower
that divides opinion
– we think
they are fun
and decorative.*

The shape of our Striped Orchid is inspired by a spider orchid flower. It grows in large parts of South and Central America and is very decorative. We have removed the spots and replaced them with hand-coloured stripes around the edges. Use these if you want to create an exotic look.

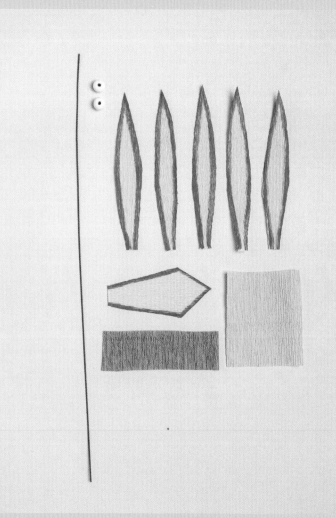

YOU WILL NEED:

1 piece of floristry wire,
L: 40cm/16in, T: 1.5mm/15ga

2 beads for the eye of the flower

Crêpe paper for the eye (centre) of the flower

5 long petals

1 short petal (the lip)

Crêpe paper to cover the stem, 140 gsm (see p. 173)

Orange artist marker to colour the edges of the petals

Brush to curve the petals

Note: The orchid has a slightly longer core, which is why we put two beads on top of each other.

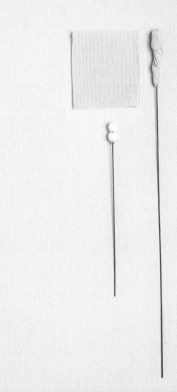

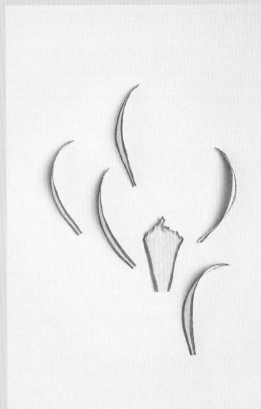

1. First, glue the two beads onto the end of the floristry wire. Once the beads are glued, cover them with crêpe paper (p. 40).

2. Now you need to shape your petals – start with the five long ones. First, draw around the edges with your orange marker pen (p. 58). Then shape the petals by curving them over a brush (p. 39). Continue until you're happy with the shape.

   Draw around the edges of the little petal with your orange marker pen. Then shape the petal by giving it three twists on each side, so the very tip of the petal curls (p. 37). Then stretch it a little bit (p. 36).

TIP } The orchids can be coloured in many different ways. You can even give them spots and choose a more muted colour combination.

3. When all the petals are ready, glue them to the middle of the flower (p. 36). Start by gluing the short petal and one of the long petals directly opposite each other. Then place two long petals facing each other between the two petals you have just glued on – the petals should form a cross when looking at the flower from above.

    Glue the final two long petals behind the short petal, so that the five long petals are evenly spaced around the eye of the flower.

4. Now all the petals have been glued on, and you can cover the floristry wire with crêpe paper (p. 50).

STRIPED ORCHID
– TEMPLATES

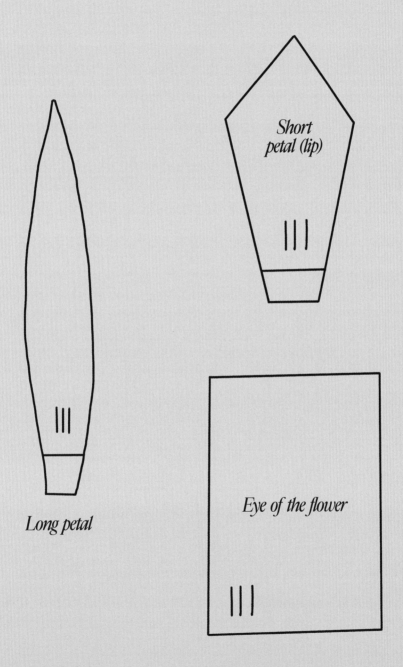

Short
petal (lip)

Long petal

Eye of the flower

A flower that attracts attention despite its simplicity.

The Almeja Flower is one of the first flowers we developed, which is why it has a special place in our hearts. The flower is quite simple, and is beautiful both alone and in a bouquet. It is also attractive when displayed on the table in its own right like in our *flora* concept (p. 201).

It you want a fuller centre in the flower, you can choose to make long stamens. The flowers can also be made larger by adding four more petals for more volume.

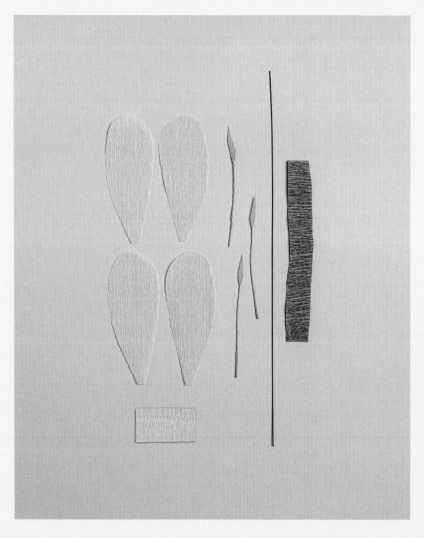

YOU WILL NEED:

1 piece of floristry wire,
L: 30cm/12in, T: 1.5mm/15ga

4 petals, 140 gsm

3 pointed stamens – 90 gsm or 140 gsm

1 piece of crêpe paper to attach the stamens together

Crêpe paper to cover the stem,
140 gsm (see p. 173)

Small container of glue and another of glitter

1. Cut and shape three pointed stamens following the technique on p. 43. To glue the stamens onto the floristry wire, first cut a small piece of crêpe paper and place it on the table. Apply a line of glue to the paper, and place the three stamens on top. Now place the end of the floristry wire on top of it all, and roll the small piece of crêpe paper around both the floristry wire and the stamens so they are held together.

2. Add glitter to the ends of the stamens by dipping the tips carefully in craft glue and then in glitter (p. 54). Set aside to dry.

3. Shape the four petals by twisting (p. 37) and stretching them (p. 36). Now the petals needs to be glued onto the floristry wire. This is done by attaching them in pairs (p. 36 and p. 47). First, glue two petals opposite each other. Then glue the other two petals opposite each other in the spaces between the first petals.

4. Cover the floristry wire with crêpe paper (p. 50) and bend it so the stem isn't straight.

ALMEJA FLOWER
– TEMPLATES

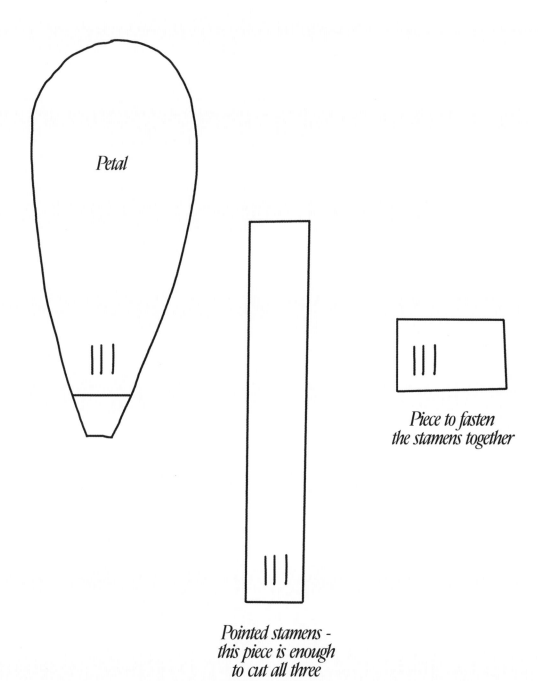

Petal

*Piece to fasten
the stamens together*

*Pointed stamens -
this piece is enough
to cut all three*

*The flowers are
impressive,
as they shoot
towards the
four corners
of the world.*

The Amaryllis is an impressive flower that consists of a sturdy stem and four beautiful flower heads. It originates from tropical parts of South Africa. A classic amaryllis is typically white, pink or deep red. We have created a less conventional variety in cream and orange tones.

This flower is excellent as part of a table setting and the only limit to how it can be used is your imagination. This flower is typically seen in Europe at Christmas, so make a dark red or cream version to use as a festive decoration or centrepiece.

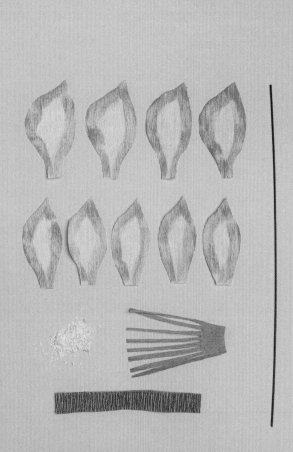

YOU WILL NEED:

1 piece of floristry wire,
L: 40cm/16in, T: 1.5mm/15ga

1 long stamen, 140 gsm

1 short stamen for confetti, 140 gsm

4 large petals, 90 gsm

5 smaller petals, 90 gsm

Crêpe paper to cover the stem,
140 gsm (see p. 173)

PanPastel in orange

Sponge

Small container of glue

If you don't have a PanPastel, you can use a marker pen (artist marker) to colour the edges. It's a good idea to cover your worktop when using PanPastels as they transfer easily.

1. Start by cutting your long stamen (p. 42).
Then glue it to your floristry wire by putting a
strip of glue on it and rolling it around the wire.

Next, make confetti for the tip of the stamen
(p. 55). Once you have cut the confetti, dip the
tips of the stamen carefully into craft glue and
then into the confetti.

Set aside to dry.

2. Now your petals need to be coloured and then
gently shaped.

First, start by colouring the edges of the petals
orange, using the sponge to dab the PanPastel
carefully along the edge of each one so it takes
the colour. The colour could be more intense
in some places, as this gives a beautiful and
dynamic look to the flower.

Continued on the following page.

Once all the edges have been coloured, the petals need to be shaped. This is done by curving them with a brush (p. 39). Note that the petals don't need to be stretched as this automatically happens when you curve them.

Now all the petals are shaped and ready to be glued onto the stem of the flower. They need to be glued with the coloured edges facing in towards the stamen.

First, take the five smaller petals and glue them in place (p. 49).

3. Then glue on the four large petals in pairs (p. 47). Glue two petals on facing each other and then the remaining two facing each other in the gaps between the first petals.

Cover the flower stem with crêpe paper (p. 50).

You can choose to make only a single flower. If you want to make four flowers that merge into one, continue to step 4.

4. If you would like a large version of our Amaryllis, you need to make four individual flowers following the previous steps. Once all four flowers are made and the stems are covered with crêpe paper, assemble them so they each point in a different direction. Then cover the join of the stems with extra crêpe paper so that they have one joined stem with four flower heads.

AMARYLLIS
– TEMPLATES

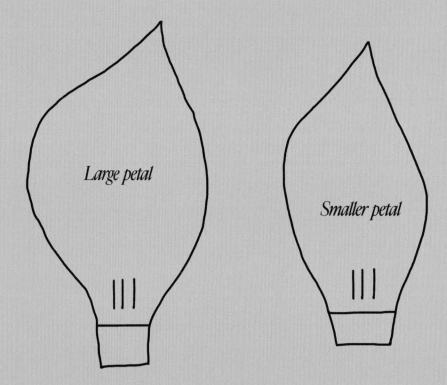

Large petal

Smaller petal

Long stamen

Short stamen for confetti

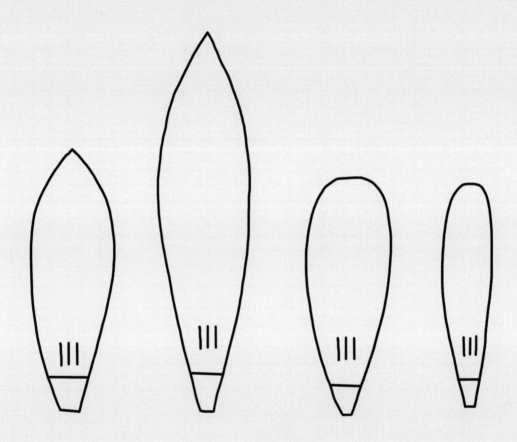

Green leaves

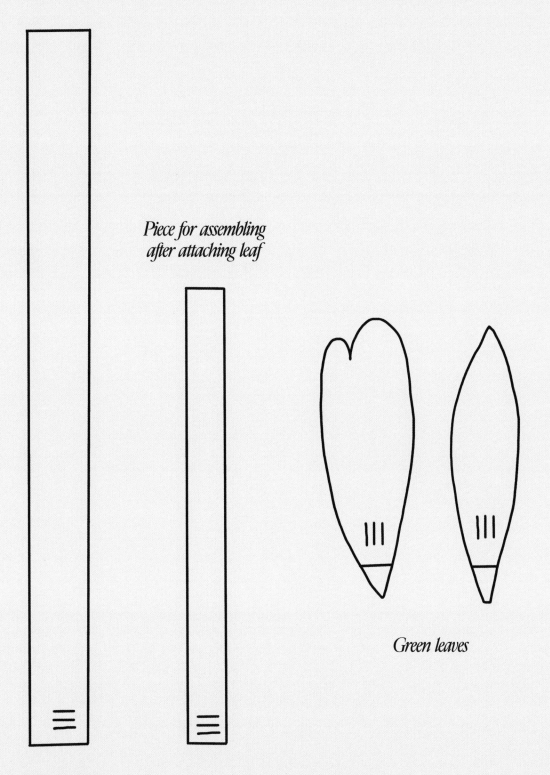

*Piece for assembling
after attaching leaf*

Green leaves

Flower stem

COLOURS AND

PAPER FLOWERS

Introduction

Colours are much more than just yellow, green and blue. Every colour is full of shades, tones and possible combinations. If you take yellow, for example, there are an infinite number of tones, starting with a very delicate light yellow, through to a more classic yellow, deep sunflower and neon yellow – and the same applies to all other colours. There is actually no end to the possibilities when working with colours.

Colours can help set a mood and tell a story, and colourful paper flowers can brighten the room and contribute to either a calm or festive atmosphere. So if you want to create even more flower magic, an obvious place to start is with colour.

At Almeja Space, colours are in everything we do. Some of the colours we work with jump out at you: tropical orange, warm pink, summer yellow, sea blue and spring green. Others are more delicate and muted, such as pale yellow, beige or sage green. Our colours are often combined with glitter or coloured confetti, which adds a hint of adventure and helps to catch the eye.

Interpretations of colours are very individual and subjective, so the next pages should be seen as our observations and understanding of colours and their meanings, as well as our ideas for how you can use them. We will also briefly introduce you to selected basic principles within colour theory.

We hope to inspire you on how you can put together different colour palettes when you start making your paper flowers.

Contrasting colours

Contrasting colours emphasize each other while creating a harmonious look. Something magical happens when the colours meet – they complement each other. When contrasting colours are put together, each of the colours seems more intense, and this is exactly why it is interesting to use them for paper flowers.

Warm and cool colours

A colour can be either warm or cool – or something in-between. So a colour can give you an instinctive feeling of either warmth or coolness. Colours such as snow white and ice blue give a calm and cool look, while sunshine yellow and flaming red can give you a feeling of energy and warmth. The colours you choose for your paper flowers are therefore very important as they need to reflect the feeling or mood you want your flowers to radiate.

You can see an example of contrasting colours on the opposite page.

What warm colours have in common is how they all have a red, yellow or golden undertone. Examples of warm colours can be the clear and bright colours that peek out during spring and completely transform the wintry look of nature with Easter yellow, grass green and even coral. Many of the colours that light up a summer's day – such as sunflower yellow and poppy red – are warm.

In the autumn, the landscape changes to the most beautiful warm colour palette of golden tones as the trees get ready for winter. All the brown, red, orange and burnt tones come together – especially earthy colours such as olive green, rust and golden yellow.

The cool colour palette is characterized by all the colours with a blue undertone, and these are most often crisp colours such as snow white, jet black and royal blue. Cooler colours experienced in the summer can be sun-kissed colours that appear more delicate and faded, such as dusty pink, muted pastels and sedate colours.

A warm, autumnal colour combination is shown on the opposite page.

Colour symbolism

Flowers come in all kinds of colours, and we each attach different meanings and feelings to them.

We love most colours here at Almeja Space, but we very often use orange, pink and yellow shades because we think they radiate joy, creativity and magic. Here's our take on what different colours signal:

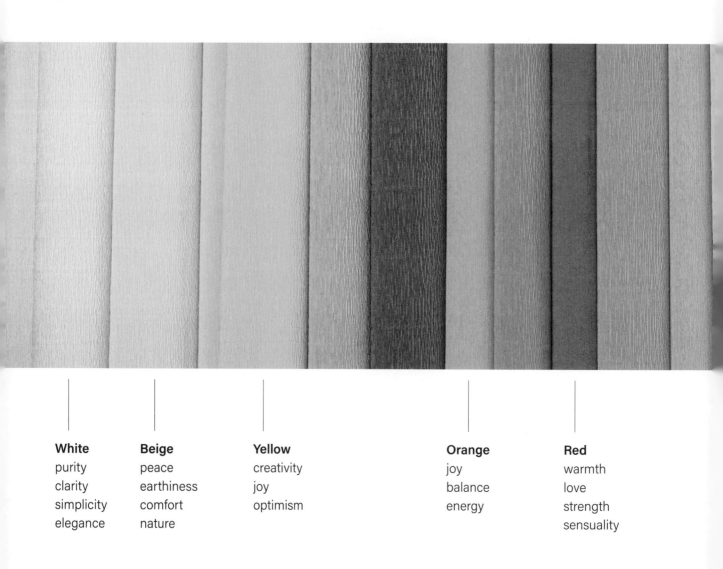

White
purity
clarity
simplicity
elegance

Beige
peace
earthiness
comfort
nature

Yellow
creativity
joy
optimism

Orange
joy
balance
energy

Red
warmth
love
strength
sensuality

Pink
elegance
power
magic

Lilac
safety
peace
warmth

Blue
harmony
peace
balance

Green
reassurance
hope
invigoration

TIP } Try making mood boards with colour
combinations. Take a large piece
of cardboard or make space on a
noticeboard and fill it with colour
samples, sketches, words, drawings,
watercolours or postcards. Choose
colours that make you happy and
evoke good vibes.

Find your colours

The colour combinations you choose for your paper flowers are, as we previously mentioned, important because they create the look and mood that your flowers radiate. We want to encourage you to create your own colour combinations based on the colours you like best and that you are drawn to. Feel free to be colourful and even challenge yourself by throwing yourself into colour combinations you wouldn't normally choose. Maybe you already know which colours you'll use – if not, you can try this little exercise:

When you need to find inspiration for your own colour combinations, an ideal place to start looking is in your wardrobe or around your home. Pay attention to which colours repeat and which colours you are drawn to. Some people love bright colours, others love more earthy colours, while others again prefer very delicate pastels or dark tones. Maybe you'll be surprised and see some colour combinations you hadn't thought of before. Make a note of your colours and use them as a starting point when you start making paper flowers.

Almeja's colour palettes

At Almeja Space, we are so lucky that our work consists of working on a number of different paper flowers in various colour palettes. When we have to put together a new colour palette, we often start with the audience or the purpose it's intended for.

Colour palettes are very important to our work, as they are one of the main elements of our floral designs. Over time, our colour palettes have changed as we have become more and more daring, venturing into new unusual combinations.

We have put together six colour palettes for you, to make it easier and more manageable when choosing colours for your flowers. The colours can be mixed and matched within each colour palette, so you can create precisely the look you want!

Kissed by the sunset

This colour combination consists of coral, pink, light yellow and amber shades. It gives a feeling of being kissed by the setting sun. Use it if you want to create a warm, cosy and playful look.

Springtime sensations

This colour combination exudes spring. It's a combination of beige, white and yellow mixed with strong coral tones, soft lilac and caramel. Use it if you want to create a soft, fresh spring look.

TIP { You can use pink crêpe paper
     { to cover your flower stems if
     { you want to create a completely
     { pastel look.

Pastels

This colour combination of light pastel colours is perfect for spring decorating – on the dining table, in a holiday home or in the bathroom.

The pale yellow, light pink, lilac and cream tones give a feeling of adventure and magic. The colours are pleasant to look at and help create a soft and calm atmosphere.

Blue skies

This colour palette works really well if you want your flowers to express tranquility and balance. The blue colours are evocative of the sky and the sea. They help to create an atmosphere of harmony, but also strength.

TIP ⟩ If you can't quite find the shade of blue you want to use in your paper flowers, you can choose to dye pale crêpe paper with blue watercolour paint to create your own colour.

Candy floss

This colour combination with various pink tones is ideal to use if you want to create a warm, fresh and welcoming feeling. We find this colour palette is very popular. The shades of pink strike a chord with most people and work well all year round.

Tropical vibes

This colour scheme radiates joy and energy. It reminds us of sunsets, tropical skies and warmth. Create balance in this look by using orange colours alongside beige tones. If you want a more energetic vibe, you can use darker and more intense orange shades mixed with delicate and pale orange tones.

DECORATING

WITH PAPER FLOWERS

Introduction

Paper flowers are extremely stylish and fun to decorate with. You can display them in many ways and use them for different purposes and occasions. For example, decorate the summer dining table with paper flowers, put them on a string and make them into a garland, or use your paper flowers to decorate other parts of the home. The only limit is your imagination.

As paper flowers naturally don't need to be watered, they work well in a holiday home, the office and in the bathroom, so there is always something decorative around you that you don't need to look after.

Since paper flowers often have a slimmer flower stem, it's a good idea to use a vase with a narrow opening. It holds the flowers together and produces a more compact bouquet.

If you would like to use a vase with a larger opening, you can pour rice into it. The rice then ensures your arrangement is secure and the flowers don't fall to one side. Sand also works well to stabilise your paper flowers so they stay where you have placed them. Rice and sand are both good alternatives to floral foam.

Arrange your flowers 'ikebana style'. Ikebana is a Japanese word for the art of arranging flowers. Ikebana focuses on the beautiful, simple and natural. Shape a little ball of chicken wire to fit the bottom of your vase. The chicken wire has lots of holes for you to place your flowers into so they are held securely.

You can also style your paper flowers in a nice clay pot. This provides a raw contrast to the fine flowers and creates a more robust look. Use rice, sand or chicken wire in the base.

We use antique kenzans (spiky flower frogs) that can be placed directly on the table. A kenzan consists of a heavy base with stainless steel needles you can insert the flowers into. They are available in different sizes.

Use your paper flowers in a holiday home. They don't need to be looked after, so there will always be decorative flowers when you return to your sanctuary.

Use paper flowers outside as decorations on sunny days. Although amaryllis are often associated with Christmas, they also work well in summer.

Paper flowers are brilliant as place-card holders. Put a name tag on a string and tie it around your paper flower. The flower can either be placed directly on the plate, or it can be twisted around the top or bottom of a glass.

Paper flowers made on thin floristry wire (0.9mm/19ga for example) also work perfectly as napkin rings. Simply fold your napkin however you like, then wrap your flower stem around it so that the flower faces upwards.

Create your own wildflower meadow with our *flora* concept by displaying the paper flowers in their own right on your table. Twist the end of the flower stem around something so it is shaped into a curl that can act as a stand. Now you can place the flower on the table.

Another idea is to make a hanging display using fishing line and around ten flowers – depending on how long the display needs to be. Tie the flowers onto the fishing line at 10–15cm/4–6in intervals. If the flowers are tricky to tie, you can glue them to the fishing line with a glue gun.

You can also use fishing line to hang your paper flowers from the ceiling at different heights – like a mobile. This can be very decorative in a bedroom or child's room and creates a lovely calm effect. Hang a paper flower from the end of a fishing line and attach the other end to the ceiling. We recommend you use 3–5 flowers.

Twist several simple flowers together so it looks like a branch, as shown below, using Almeja Flowers.

Give paper flowers as a hostess gift – a personal and unique gesture.

TIP ⟩ When making a bouquet, it's best to put an odd number of flowers together. There is something special about the numbers 3, 5, 7 and 9, which create a certain harmony and balance in a bouquet.

Simple bouquet

Mixed bouquet

Single-coloured bouquet

Wild-flower bouquet

Decorating with paper flowers　203

Index

More from Almeja Space

You can further immerse yourself
in our universe here:

Instagram:
@almejaspace

Website:
almeja-space.com

Webshop:
almeja-space.com/papirblomster-kits

Workshops:
almeja-space.com/workshop-papirblomster

A special thanks

We couldn't have completed this wild project
without our lovely family: our supportive husbands,
our caring mum, inventive dad and Sine's sweet
daughter.

Our cheerleaders in the form of our good friends and
network who we have been able to bounce ideas off.

Writing a book requires a team. We have had some
super-cool women with us for the creative process:

Our editor, Julie, has managed the process and made
sure we met deadlines while keeping the quality and
our spirits high.

Our photographer, Karyna Bila, has been so
dedicated and invested since day one. She has shot
over 600 images that we have styled. The results
have been magical.

Our graphic designer, Louise Jacobsen, has played
with colours, fonts and the placement of our many
crazy ideas.

Finally, we couldn't have made this book without
each other and our courage to embark on this
creative adventure together.

First published as *Papirblomster med Almeja Space*
Copyright © Sara Finne Frandsen & Sine Finne Frandsen
and Lindhardt & Ringhof A/S 2022

This English language edition published in 2024 by
Quadrille, an imprint of Hardie Grant Publishing,
in agreement with Bennet Agency

Quadrille
52–54 Southwark Street, London SE1 1UN
quadrille.com

Managing Director Sarah Lavelle
Senior Commissioning Editor Harriet Butt
Assistant Editor Oreolu Grillo
Original Cover and Graphic Designer Louise Jacobsen
Designer Sarah Fisher
Head of Production Stephen Lang
Senior Production Controller Katie Jarvis

Cataloguing in Publication Data: a catalogue record
for this book is available from the British Library.

Text © Sara Finne Frandsen and Sine Finne Frandsen 2024
Design © Quadrille 2024
Photography © Karyna Bila 2024 except for pp. 8–9
Anitta Behrendt 2024

ISBN 978 1 8378 3169 2
Printed in China using soy inks

MIX
Paper | Supporting
responsible forestry
FSC
www.fsc.org
FSC™ C020056